Ted Greene
MODERN CHORD PROGRESSIONS

Alfred Music
P.O. Box 10003
Van Nuys, CA 91410-0003
alfred.com

Copyright © MCMLXXVI, MMIX by Alfred Music
All rights reserved

No part of this book shall be reproduced, arranged, adapted, recorded, publicly performed, stored in a retrieval system,
or transmitted by any means without written permission from the publisher. In order to comply with copyright laws, please apply for
such written permission and/or license by contacting the publisher at alfred.com/permissions.

ISBN-10: 0-89898-698-2
ISBN-13: 978-0-89898-698-3

ACKNOWLEDGEMENTS

I would like to express a warm thanks to the following people for their help in creating this book or getting me to the place where I could write it:

For paste-up and lay-out: Tony Mandracchia, Bruce Diehl, and Jim Tyler.

For typesetting: Bob Campbell.

For proof-reading: Peter Butterfield, Dale Zdenek, and my mother.

For their musical influence: Many fine guitarists and musicians but especially the incredible George Van Eps, the late Wes Montgomery, one of my teachers-Jay Lacy, and three great "chordal" guitarists from Canada . . . Domenic Troiano, Lenny Breau, and Ed Bickert.

Many fine musical authors, such as those listed in the back of this book.

But most of all, the many composers and songwriters whose indirect help, through their music, has been a true blessing and a tremendous source of enjoyment, education and inspiration. Some who have touched me the most, especially in relation to the material in this book, are: J. S. Bach, Claude Debussy, Max Steiner, Richard Rodgers, George Gershwin, Sammy Fain, Jule Styne, Jerome Kern, James Van Heusen, Vernon Duke, Cole Porter, Harold Arlen, Neal Hefti, Henry Mancini, Burt Bacharach and Antonio Carlos Jobim.

For their highly appreciated musical encouragement: Klaus Lendzian, my sister Linda, Michael Smith, Chips Hoover, Tom Jones, and Jay Graydon.

For helping create the necessary incentive to write this information down: All of my interested students and my friend and publisher, Dale Zdenek.

And finally, a very special thanks to my parents, whose patience, love and assistance have been far above and beyond the plane of goodness — to them I lovingly dedicate this book.

TABLE OF CONTENTS

MODERN CHORD PROGRESSIONS   VOLUME I

INTRODUCTION

When I was first learning to play the guitar, my teacher would come to my house and, if I recall correctly, the routine went something like this: He would enter the house, say hello, ask me if I had practiced (I would lie and say "yes" or be more truthful and say "a little"), and then say "Let me see the box" (no kidding—this is what he said and, now that I think of it, my first guitar did look something like a box). Anyway, he would take my guitar, tune it, and then play a little chord progression which would just floor me. Needless to say, the chords and progressions he would play were quite a few notches above the simple sounds like C to G7 that I was struggling with, and I just figured that the things he was doing were light years away for me.

Well, at some stage of the game I received my first chord book and, in a short time, I remember becoming very disappointed with it because, although the book was teaching me some good chord forms, there were no nice chord progressions; there were no little passages that sounded like music; instead, there were just exercises, where you took the same chord form and moved it up one fret at a time, in order to learn the names of the form on the different frets. While exercises can be very helpful, most people also like to be able to play something that sounds like music, to give them an incentive to practice; and if that something can be the vehicle by which they acquire a good portion of their musical education as well, it seems right to expose them to such material, doesn't it?

As you might gather, I sincerely feel that this book, and the succeeding volumes, offer you the opportunity to become friends with just such sounds — sounds that will not only delight your ears but will, when analyzed carefully, enrich your understanding of some of the glories of this phenomenon that we call music.

It must be pointed out that this book is not for the complete beginner. If you fall into this category, it is to your great advantage to find a good teacher (ask around but shop carefully, as you would before any major investment) — he or she will speed up the learning process and help you to avoid the creation of bad habits. Later, after you are able to play the basic chords (you will learn the basic chords from almost any guitar teacher in the world), you will be ready to tackle this book. Also, in order to most fully understand this book, you will have to have a knowledge of the fundamentals of music theory (like scales, intervals, keys, key signatures, triads, inversions, and seventh chords). This information can be acquired, again, from a good teacher or from one of the many books on the subject (see recommended list near the back of this book). The reason that this information is not included in the present volume is that it really requires a whole book in itself if the student wants to thoroughly know these fundamentals and, unfortunately, this is the only way to go if you want to really understand music — it is well worth the time and effort, so start as soon as you can, and get it out of the way.

One bright spot — even if you don't understand what's going on as far as the theory aspect of this book is concerned, you will still benefit in quite a few ways if you begin practicing the examples given while you are simultaneously catching up on music theory. Some of these benefits are: 1) You will be training and developing your fingers, 2) Developing your musical ear (by coming into contact with musical examples), and 3) Sharpening your knowledge of the guitar fingerboard (at least learning where all those weird chords like C speckled 9th are, even if you don't know why some of them have, say, a fermented fifth yet). Eventually, if you keep working faithfully at your study of music theory, understanding will enter the picture, and you will experience the joy of knowing, of not only being able to see where everything is coming from, but of being able to make up your own variations using the principles involved.

You may be wondering what a "modern" chord progression is. Ask ten different musicians and see what they say. Probably the only thing that most of them will agree about is that it's pretty hard to define this concept. So why did I use this title? Well, the progressions in these books form the backbone for much of the music written in the 20th century, so it didn't seem too far off base to use the word "modern". However, I must confess to having thrown in some examples in the styles of some earlier eras in music; this was done, quite frankly, with the hope of inspiring you to delve more deeply into a study of the wonderful sounds left for us by our musical ancestors. There is tremendous value, on many levels, in such a study, and you can be sure that the rewards will repay you many times over for the necessary time and energy spent.

Another good question that you may be asking is, "Where does one use all these progressions?" Although this depends to some extent on the individual, there are certain areas that most musicians are interested in; some of these areas are:

1. **Improvising** — Whether you want to improvise with others or by yourself, you will probably find the going quite a bit easier, in almost any type of music, if you have a knowledge of chord progressions.

2. **Composing** — While you may be fortunate enough to be able to write songs or pieces by "ear", the ear can only take you so far. There are many sounds that you may not have dreamed even existed or, if you did know of them, maybe you didn't have the foggiest idea about where to look for them or how they were derived. Once you understand the principles of chord progressions, whole new worlds of sound will open up for your use and enjoyment.

3. **"Recomposing"** — This deals with taking someone else's song or piece and working it out in your own style. As you might guess, a knowledge of progressions is priceless here also.

4. **Arranging** — Very similar to recomposing, but you might also wish to arrange your own song or piece. Virtually every good arranger understands about progressions and makes use of them in introductions, "fills", harmonizations of melodies, modulation passages, and endings.

Earlier it was mentioned that your musical ear will be sharpened if you practice the material in this book; this is true in at least a twofold way: Not only will your ability to select and hear sounds for your own playing improve, but in a like manner, your ability to recognize what others are doing (on records, tapes, live performances, radio, etc.), will grow, slowly but surely, or if you work harder, even by leaps and bounds.

There is a strong emphasis on melody throughout the entire book and if you study all the examples, you can be confident that your feeling for melody in general, and for melodic variations on chord progressions, will be in pretty good shape.

Many of the examples can be applied to different rhythms (such as jazz-waltz, swing, bossa-nova and others); if you have trouble in this area, a good teacher might be your best bet again.

You will probably find that quite a few of the examples in this book will not be as easy to play as you would like them to be — in fact, some may even seem impossible at first, causing you to grace my name with a few four-letter titles. DON'T GIVE UP! Remember how hard barre chords were at first? How is it that you can play them now? One magic word: PRACTICE. You don't get something for nothing on the guitar, but Nature has a way of stretching and reshaping your hands if you meet her halfway. Even a person with small hands, who is willing to practice, will be able to play these examples (don't be alarmed at cramps, calluses and other assorted aches and pains . . . they're all part of the learning process).

Key words: PATIENCE and DETERMINATION.

If you encounter any progression that sounds at all strange or unattractive to you, make sure you are really playing all the right notes, and then play it a couple of more times. Many times your ear will adjust to something that, upon first hearing, sounded a little "out in the twinkies", and you may even begin to really like some of these sounds. (Some people who do not respond very favorably to modern chords at first, acquire a passionate love for them, with continued exposure.)

Actually, it is a good habit to repeat every progression, no matter what your feelings are toward it, because there is a strong possibility that you will hear new things in there each time (every chord progression is really a collection of melodies being heard simultaneously, and your ears might latch on to different ones of these melodies at different times).

It is highly recommended that you go through this book in order, thoroughly absorbing the principles and at least some of the examples in each section before moving on to the next. The book is laid out in such a fashion that this is the only way to get the most out of it; if you skip around, you are doing yourself an injustice; the reasons for this will only be clear after you have gone through the book in order.

As you play through the progressions, you will probably wonder why many of them are so short. There is good reason for this. If you were to analyze the chord progressions of many different songs or "classical" pieces, you would notice that the same short progressions keep appearing over and over again but in different combinations with each other, and these short chord progression combinations form much of the bulk of these songs or pieces. To be sure, there are some longer progressions that are commonly used, and these will be covered as well (mainly in Volumes 2 and 3). But even these longer progressions are often derived from the shorter progressions, so we can and should consider these common short progressions to be our essential building blocks. You may be asking, "How will I learn how to combine all these progressions?" Good question. Mainly by experimenting and/or using the principles to be given in Volumes 2 and 3, not to mention learning by observing how others have dealt or are dealing with the subject.

The short progressions are systematically arranged according to certain concepts which will become clear as you go; these progressions utilize virtually all of the most important chord forms and the entire fingerboard, while offering enough variations so that, in all likelihood, you will have little desire or need to create more, even though you will be thoroughly able to. The longer progressions are less systematic, while not being totally without logic that you will be able to relate to. In case you are curious, systematic variation techniques on these longer progressions will be given in Volume 2.

Finally, while it is absolutely in your best interest to play through all the examples given, don't feel as though you have to spend your time memorizing all of them; this is neither necessary nor desirable because your time is precious and you don't need to know, say, three hundred different ways to play the same progression before you can start working on another. You will naturally want to memorize some of your favorites though and please remember that the short progressions are eventually going to be combined with each other, as well as with longer progressions, and with other harmonic tools.

Sincerely hoping that this book, and its brothers to follow, will be stimulating, rewarding and enjoyable.

Ted Greene

HOW TO INTERPRET THE DIAGRAMS

The type of diagrams used in this book are the standard ones used for guitar. The following points are given with the hope of clearing up any confusion on how to read them:

The vertical lines are the strings; the horizontal lines are the frets.

2. The fret that the chord is to be played on is indicated by a number to the left of the diagram. Example:

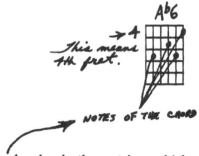

3. The dots (darkened-in circles) in the diagrams are the notes of the chord and only those strings which contain notes are to be played — in other words, your right hand should only pluck those particular strings that have the dots.

4. Speaking of pluck, the progressions in this book were geared to be played without a flat pick, that is, they are meant to be played using only the thumb and fingers of the right hand (however, if you are accustomed to using a thumb pick or finger picks or both, this book is also right up your alley). Now maybe many of you have never played with your fingers up till now and might be hesitant to learn. There is nothing to fear — sure it will be awkward for a week or two but the benefits that follow soon after this, far outweigh the initial period of discomfort. The two main benefits are: 1) the ability to play all the notes in a chord at the same time; most people find the sound produced by this technique to be very attractive; 2) the availability of many new chords that are very impractical when approached with just a flat pick. One bonus of playing finger-style: Once you have gotten used to it, the sensation of your fingers grabbing the strings on four or five-note chords just feels great.

Okay, so how do you go about getting into this type of right hand technique if you are a complete beginner at it? A few simple guidelines are all you really need:

a. Your thumb (T) should strike the lowest (thickest) string involved in the chord; your other fingers just get added on "in order" (starting with the 1st finger) according to how many other notes are in the chord. Examples:

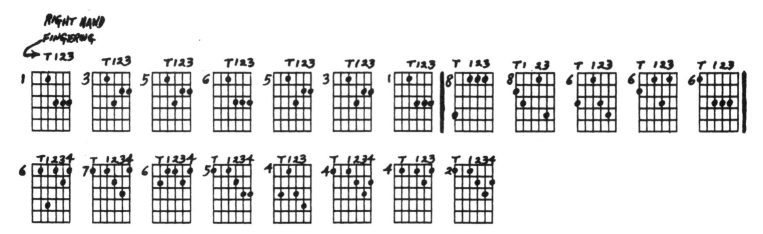

Don't be alarmed if you can't quite play these examples yet; the main thing right now is to understand how you will use your right hand in plucking the strings.

b. Almost all guitarists who use their bare thumb and fingers for plucking have found it necessary to let their nails grow here so as to produce a clearer and cleaner sound.

c. Holding your right wrist up away from the guitar puts your fingers into a position where it is easier to achieve good tone, accuracy and speed. This posture may seem a little awkward at first (mainly because it's new to you) but gradually this becomes an incredibly relaxed way to play. As far as how high to hold the wrist, just start out with a moderate height (about 2 to 3 inches) and gradually you will find yourself going up higher automatically (although at first, you will probably keep tending to go lower if you don't keep a pretty constant eye on the situation). Incidentally, if you play with a thumb pick, you won't be able to hold your wrist up as far and, in fact, you may not find it desirable to hold your wrist up at all; experiment and see what you think.

d. As far as the actual plucking of the strings goes, all you need to do is "squeeze" gently to produce a sound. Exceptions to this arise when dealing with a chord that has six notes in it. In such a case, one recommended approach is to just use your thumb to strum all the strings.

4. Optional notes will be symbolized by ——————→ [diagram] instead of [diagram] If optional notes are given, it's worth your while to investigate the subtle differences that result from their inclusion. If more than one optional note is given, try all possible combinations.

5. Open strings will be symbolized by a dot "above" the diagram if the diagram is on the 1st fret (as at left). If a diagram were on, say, the 4th fret and a note was above the diagram, this note would be on the 3rd fret, not open, unless otherwise indicated.

Example: [diagram labeled OPEN STRINGS]

6. In many chords, more than one good fingering is possible (referring to the left hand now); but in certain progressions, some fingerings are definitely more advantageous than others and so in these cases, if there was a reasonable degree of doubt as to whether or not you would readily see the best fingering, it was written below the diagram. Example:

[diagrams with fingerings: 2 34, 2 34, 2 341, 2 341, 1 342 ← LEFT HAND FINGERING]

Sometimes the "best" fingering will only prove so in the long run and you might think it is the worst fingering at first, causing you to jump to an erroneous assumption about the marital status of my parents at the time of my birth. But have faith, the fingering is there for a good reason and has been successfully tested with students.

By the way, concerning left hand fingering: The index finger is considered to be the first finger, the middle finger is the second, and so on; if the thumb were to be used, it would be indicated by a T.

6

7. ⌣←This symbol between two notes of two different diagrams means that you should hold the note and let it ring but not pluck it again in the second diagram (in other words, let the note SUSTAIN from one chord to the next; this will make sense when you encounter this type of situation).

8. When you see symbols with the 2nd or 3rd finger on two adjacent strings, this is often going to require you to use a special technique that we will call the <u>double stop</u>. We can define the double stop as a technique where you come down with the tip of your finger right <u>between two strings</u>, so as to sound them both. Unless you are lucky enough to have wide fingers already, this is not going to work out too well at first (sound familiar?) <u>However</u>, (here he goes again), just keep on practicin' — Magically enough, more skin will appear on the tips of your fingers, enabling you to successfully execute these double stops. A good way to speed up your development in this area is to practice on a classical (nylon string) guitar; as you probably know, the fingerboard is much wider and the strings are farther apart than on other types of guitars. This will make it even <u>harder</u> to cope with double stops, but somehow this is good. Whatever it is that produces more skin will produce it faster when it keeps receiving signals that you are in dire need of help; also there are some good psychological reasons, that need not be explained here, for occasionally practicing on a classical guitar.

There are certain types of cases where you have the 2nd, 3rd or even the 4th finger covering two adjacent strings, but in which you will find that it is more advantageous to <u>flatten</u> your finger across both strings instead of trying to come down between them in the manner of the double stop.

Examples

A general guideline for deciding when to flatten and when to double stop might be something like: If the two adjacent notes are at the <u>top</u> of the chord (in terms of <u>pitch</u>), use the flattening technique; if they are in the bass or towards the bottom of the chord, then use the double stop. However, to help you, double stop fingerings will actually be notated with a little connecting line to distinguish them from the flattening technique: ⌐

Example:

Oh yes, don't be discouraged if you always have trouble double-stopping on the classical guitar; it will always be pretty much of a battle on the wide neck, but it will serve to make the technique surprisingly easy on the electric guitar, which is, quite frankly, the instrument that this book is most suited for. During all this talk about double stops you may have asked yourself, "Why does this nut want me to use these things, anyway?" or "What good will they do me?" Fair enough; you deserve some answers to these — some of the most important benefits of the double stop technique are: 1) the ability to play chords that could not be played any other way, 2) the ability to play some chords on higher frets than would normally be practical, and 3) the freeing of an extra finger, which can be used for certain melodic effects while you sustain the chord (more on this to come).

9. It is very important to always strive for <u>cleanliness</u> in all chords; by cleanliness, it is meant that all notes which are supposed to be sounding should be doing just that. Obvious, you say? Maybe so, but it has been my experience that it is easy to deceive yourself on this matter by taking it for granted. For instance, suppose you are given the following chord:

Let us suppose that you try and play it but, for some reason, you either miss or muffle the note on the fourth string, thereby producing the following sound:

Now, this chord has a nice sound to the ear, but it is <u>not</u> what was intended; if you are aware, as you play this chord, that something is not quite right, then you will go back and with a little extra practice, correct the problem. But the big danger lies in <u>not even realizing</u> that an error exists. (You won't ever correct a problem if you don't know that it is there to begin with.) If your ear cannot detect these errors yet, try <u>arpeggiating</u> (holding the chord down and plucking each note of the chord one at a time) chords and progressions to check your accuracy. Eventually, there will be no need for this, as you will be able to tell whether or not you are making the intended sounds, but until this happens, make it a habit to check yourself quite often.

10. If you encounter a diagram with indications for one finger on two different frets, don't be alarmed; this is what George Van Eps calls the 5th finger principle, and you can be sure that it is practical. Here is an example:

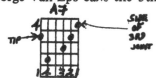

To perform this technique, the tip of your finger gets one note, and the side of the 3rd joint of the finger gets the other; in the case illustrated here, the tip of your 1st finger gets the bass note (A) while the side of the 3rd joint of your 1st finger gets the G# note on the 1st string. Compared to some of the other techniques you have already learned on the guitar, this one is relatively easy.

11. In order to indicate moving melodic lines with a sustained chord, the following symbols are used: The symbol x indicates a note that is added to the chord, after the chord has been sounded, and while the chord is still ringing (try not to muffle any of the ringing chord notes while you bring in this new note). Example:

In this diagram, your right hand would pluck the 6th, 4th and 3rd strings together and, while they were still ringing, you would pluck the 5th string - 7th fret (E). It would look like this in music notation:

Sometimes you may wish to muffle the string you have just "come from". Example:

This C note and the B note (x) might tend to clash (this is a matter of personal taste) to your ears, so in placing the 4th finger on the B note, you may choose to lightly brush against the 2nd string, thereby stopping the sound of the C note.

However in a situation like the following, you will probably agree that the C note and B♭ note (x) sound great, when ringing together. So experiment in cases like these and just let your ears be the final judge.

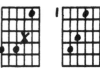

If more than one x appears in a diagram, hit all the x's together (after the chord). Example:

If an x appears on top of a regular note X, first include the note as part of the chord and then treat it as an x. Example:

The symbol □ indicates a note to be played <u>after</u> an x. Example:

As with x's, if more than one □ appears, play them together (after the x's).

Any progressions which contain melodies that are more complicated than what has been discussed so far, will be indicated in musical notation only (no diagrams). This situation will not arise in Volume 1. If left hand fingerings are indicated in a diagram which contains x's or □'s, these fingerings indicate the initial chord sound only unless otherwise indicated.

The naming of chords with x's is really debatable. For instance:

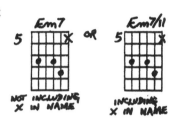

Both approaches are fine and you will see both of them used, so don't expect consistency here. Why? Because as you will see, there are times when one approach would be ridiculous, and vice versa.
Example:

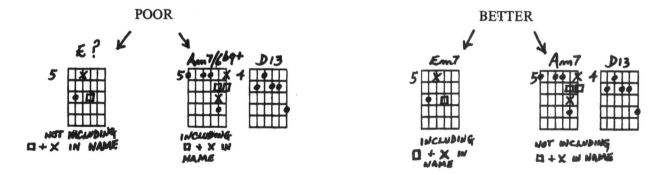

Most situations are toss-ups though as far as the naming goes, so be flexible.
If you are ever writing your own examples, it's not worth splitting hairs over.

12. You won't have much trouble understanding the names of chords, but a few points should be mentioned: a) a slash through a number means major (Example: ⁊ = Major 7th); b) + means sharped 5th unless it comes before 11 (+11) in which case it means sharped 11th; c) sus.is an abbreviation for the word suspended which means that the 3rd has been replaced with the 4th (it also has another meaning but you needn't worry about it in this book).

HOW TO MEMORIZE CHORDS

During the course of this book you will probably encounter quite a few chords that you have never played before, and you might wonder if there is a quick way to memorize them. Yes and no. While the learning process never seems to go as quickly as we would like it to, there <u>are</u> a few things that might speed it up a bit for you:

1. Many guitar players learn new chords quickly by relating them <u>visually</u> to chords they already know. Example: Suppose you encounter the following chord for the first time 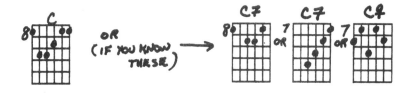 and after playing it, you

decide that you like the sound enough to want to memorize it. Suggestion: try relating it visually to:

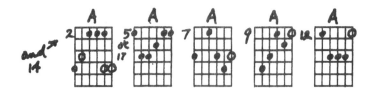

You can probably see that this type of operation will work well <u>if you already know quite a few chords</u>. Now let's suppose you don't; here is a simplified version of the same thing (quite a few players also use this approach):

2. Divide the neck up into five main areas for any major or minor chord and use these areas as reference points for any chord that you learn. For instance, using the A major chord as a model, the five areas would be:

Now suppose you encounter this chord for the first time: You could relate it to the 4th area easily.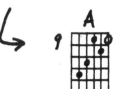

Or suppose you encounter the following: 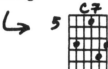   This can be easily related to the first area (transposed to C)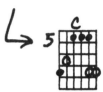

There will be chords that don't seem to neatly fall into one area, such as:

A chord such as this can be related to one of two areas or both of them: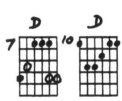

Dominant 7th type chords can be related to the major chord areas:

Suppose you encounter this chord for the first time: 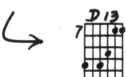   it goes with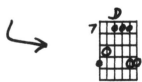

Diminished and augmented chords are more easily learned by the third technique (given below) or by some other method of your own devising.

The five main areas for minor chords are (using Am as a model):

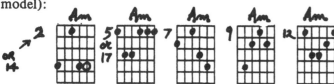

Another good technique for learning chords is:

3. Remember the chord by where the <u>root</u> is; this way assumes that: a) there is a root in the chord somewhere; b)you are able to locate it; and c) you know the names of the notes on the fingerboard. For instance, suppose you have never learned this chord:

but you have decided that you would like to so that you can use it as a reference in the five-area concept. The root in this chord is on the 4th string, so if you know the names of your notes on the 4th string, you will be able to transpose it and memorize it fairly easily by focusing on the root as a visual anchor point. This technique takes practice but it works very well, especially as a last resort when the other techniques don't seem to be doing the job. But remember to effectively use this, you should know the note names on the fingerboard. (To learn this, you might wish to make up drills like: "Find the A notes on each string; likewise with B, C, D, etc.; then A♭, B♭, etc., then A#, B#, etc." or any other drill you can think up that seems effective; or you can work on your note reading — this too will eventually teach you the note names on the finger-board — see recommended book list at end of this volume.)

Most players use a combination of all three methods outlined here, so experiment with all of them and you will find what works best for you.

HOMONYMS

Webster's dictionary defines the word <u>homonym</u> as "a word with the same pronunciation as another but with a different meaning." In other words, the two words <u>sound</u> the same but come from different places (like read and reed or principal and principle). In playing through this book, you are going to encounter <u>chord homonyms</u>, that is, chords that sound the same but have different origins and names. For instance:

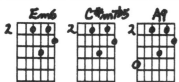

So which name is right for this chord? It depends on the situation.

If you are working with the progression, say, Em Am, and you see this chord being used in place of Em, guess what it's going to be called (how about Em6?).

Likewise, if you are working with C#m7 F#7 Bm and you run into this chord being used in place of C#m7, you can expect it to be named C#m7♭5.

Finally if you are working with Em7 A7 D and you find this chord being used in place of A7, then it will be called A9.

So, as you can see, the naming of homonyms will be determined by "what is easiest" or just plain common sense. (However, it must be mentioned that there are advantages in sometimes going with a name other than the one dictated by common sense. These advantages have to do with advanced chord substitution concepts and wandering into related keys, but they will have to be covered later.)

Memorizing a chord form with more than one name (such as the above) might be a little confusing at first, but if you apply the principles given in the section "How to Memorize Chords," you will do just fine after awhile. You <u>will</u> have to know all the useful names for a chord form or you will just be making it hard for yourself in the long run.

DIATONIC CHORD PROGRESSIONS IN MAJOR KEYS

Some of the most common chord progressions are those using only chords derived from a major scale. Because of their beauty and the bright, happy sound they produce, thousands and thousands of musicians have been attracted to these progressions. Also, from a theoretical standpoint, they are very important because they form the foundations for many of the advanced sounds that arise out of certain substitution principles.

The following information is given to make sure that you, first of all, know just what chords can be built using only the notes of a major scale (the Key of C will be used for demonstration purposes but the information can be transposed to all other keys too). In other words, every chord in the following list contains only notes that are found in the C major scale. These chords are said to be DIATONIC to the key of C (in this book, diatonic means: using only notes of the scale). You will already know much of this information (remember this book assumes that you understand the basic fundamentals of music theory — see the Introduction if you missed this point), but if there are some chords in this list that perplex you as to their construction, rest assured that if you analyze the chord forms (chord form here means the same thing as chord diagram) you will meet in this book, you will understand the construction of virtually any chord.

Analyze, as used here, means to find out what tones of the chord are present and accounted for (many chord forms leave out 5ths or roots or even other tones sometimes).

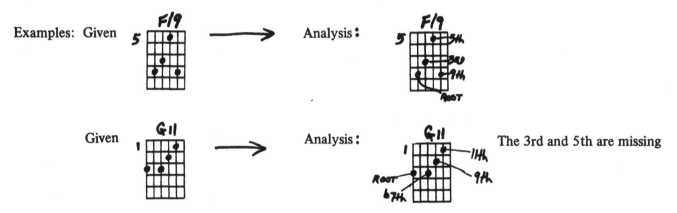

Two questions you might have at this point: 1) "How do I know what tones are supposed to be in an 11th chord (or any other chord, for that matter) to begin with?" and 2) "How do I know what tones can be left out of any chord?"

The answers to the first question can be gotten from, you guessed it . . . a good teacher; or from my first book, CHORD CATASTROPHE (also known as CHORD CHEMISTRY), amongst other books. However, if you cannot afford either of these alternatives at the moment, just remember that chords are built in 3rd intervals (if you are still asking "What's a 3rd interval?", I'm afraid that you will have to get a teacher and/or some basic theory books, as explained in the Introduction).

CHORDS BY 3rd INTERVALS

Triads — 1 3 5	11ths — 1 3 5 7 9 11	
7ths — 1 3 5 7	13ths — 1 3 5 7 9 11 13	— Very general view
9ths — 1 3 5 7 9		

The answer to the second question can be found through sheer observation. As you progress through this book, you will see many chords with "missing" tones; many chords that have missing tones are used to create smooth VOICE LEADING (voice leading is the art of connecting each note of a given chord with each note in a following chord. See CHORD CHEMISTRY — Section 13.)

EL 2779

Usually these missing tones are either the 5th or the root, as mentioned before, but don't be shocked if any other tone is left out. The main thing to concern yourself with is learning good sounding chord forms, and learning how to use them, and these two points are what this book is about.

Anyway, on with the show . . .

The diatonic triads in the key of C are: C Dm Em F G Am B^O

The diatonic 7th chords in the key of C are: C7 Dm7 Em7 F7 G7 Am7 Bm7b5

A complete list of the most commonly used diatonic chords in the key of C including the EXTENSIONS (extensions are chords that add other diatonic notes on to the diatonic triads or diatonic 7th chords) is: (capital Roman numerals indicate a major triad)

I: C, C7, C6, C/9, C6/9, C9, C13, (C7/6, Csus, C/9sus)

ii: Dm, Dm7, Dm7/11, Dm/9, Dm9, Dm11, (Dm7/6, Dm6, Dm sus)

iii: Em, Em7, Em7/11, (Em7b9, Em sus, Em7+)

IV: F, F7, F6, F/9, F6/9, F9, F13, F/9+11, F6/9+11, F7+11, F9+11, (F7/6, F/+11, F13+11)

V: G, G7, G7/6, G9, G13, G7sus, G9sus (usually called G11), G13sus, G7/6sus, Gsus, G7/11, G6

vi: Am, Am7, Am7/11, Am/9, Am9, Am11, (Am+, Amsus, Am/9sus, Am7+)

vii: B^O, Bm7b5, Bm7b5/11, Bm7/11 (no 5th), (Bm7b5#5)

also called B½ diminished 7th and written like Bø7 — both symbols will be used in this book.

These chords can be and have been combined in countless ways; for instance, in the Baroque period of music (roughly 1600-1750), mostly triads and to a lesser extent, 7th chords, suspensions and added 9ths were used. Example:

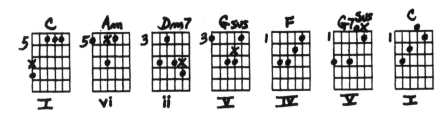

In modern times, the 7ths and extensions are used very often, with the triads playing a lesser role. Example:

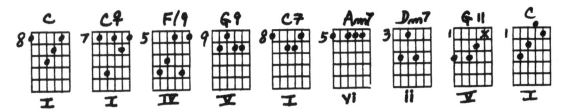

You may have noticed in examining the Roman Numeral symbols under these two progressions that the numbers I vi ii V and IV V I appear in both; these are two examples of what we will call HARMONIC FORMULAS (meaning progressions, that because they are so well liked, are constantly used by musicians as a basis for improvisation, composition, arranging and what have you). As you can imagine, it is very important to be well acquainted with harmonic formulas, and part of the function of this book will be to cover this aspect of the study of chord progressions, in great detail. The first one we are going to work with is: I iii IV V (I). Only triad symbols will be used for diatonic harmonic formulas (in other words, even if a progression uses, say C/9 Em7 F/9 G7sus C7, in a general sense it is still I iii IV V I, even though specifically it is I/9 iii7 IV/9 V7sus I7).

14

The examples in this book will only be given in one key each, but it is important to be able to play them in all keys (where this is physically possible); so it is a good idea to at least transpose your favorites into all the keys. However, some chords, especially some very modern voicings coming up later, sound pretty terrible in low registers (that is, on the lower frets) so let your ears be the guide in determining how low to take any progression (if you don't understand this, you will when you encounter the problem).

I iii IV V (I)

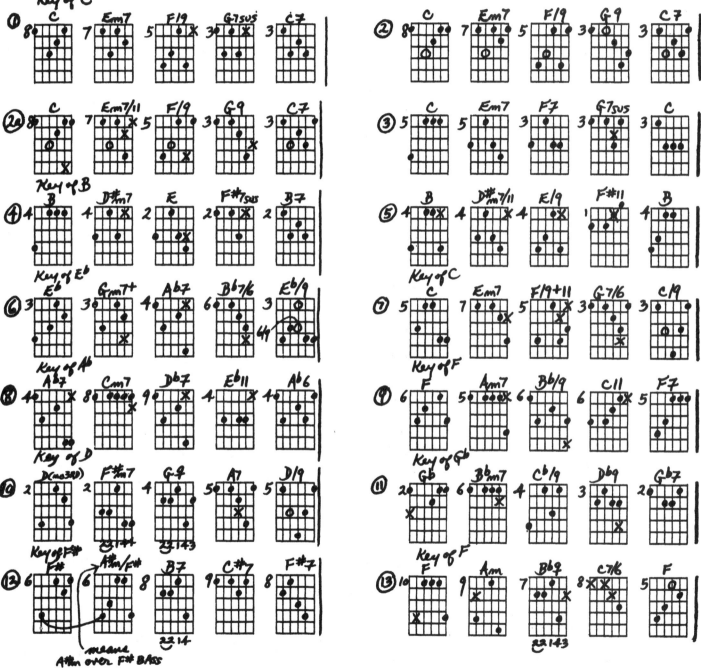

ii can substitute for IV because they are virtually the same chord — like F#m7 = A6 (the homonym concept).

16

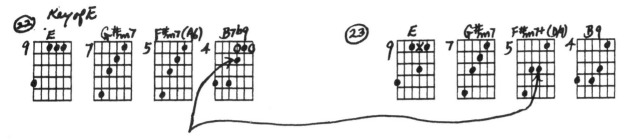

Occasionally a non-diatonic note will be thrown in for color; they will be discussed later.

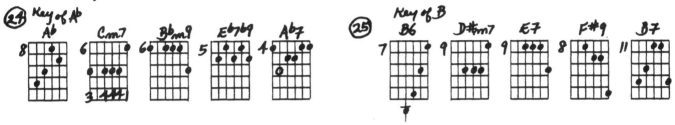

CAUTION : It is important to **THINK** when you are first learning any chord progression to get the information to sink in. The two things to think about when playing chord progressions, chord scales (to be discussed below) or what have you, are: 1) The **names** of the chords, and 2) the *"numbers"* (like I iii IV V). It won't be easy at first, but in the **long** run, you will be able to do more, be more creative if you can play **and think** together.

DIATONIC CHORD SCALES AND STRING TRANSFERENCE

Play the following:

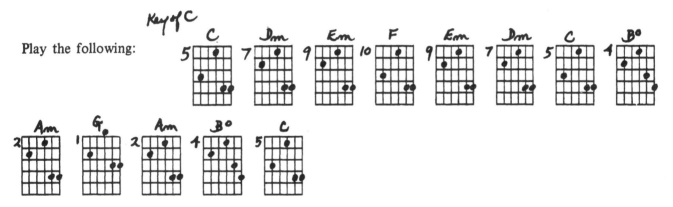

This is what will be referred to as a DIATONIC CHORD SCALE in a major key (C in this case) — for short, we will just call it a CHORD SCALE, the diatonic part being understood. By the way, why is it diatonic in the first place? Because only notes of the major scale are used, right? If this is not clear to you, don't go any further until you have cleared it up, by yourself or with the help of someone else.

Anyway, a chord scale can be built by starting on a major chord and MOVING EACH NOTE IN THE CHORD UP TO THE NEXT NOTE IN THE MAJOR SCALE WHICH HAS THE SAME NAME AS THE CHORD. For instance, in the above example, the C chord contains the following notes (from the bass up): E C G C; to find the next diatonic chord in the chord scale, the E moves up to F, the C to D, the G to A, and the C to D, thereby forming the Dm chord. If you continue the same procedure, the notes of the Dm would move up (in the C major scale) to form the Em chord and these in turn would move up to form the F chord and so on. At this stage of the game you might be saying, "So, what's the big deal? I already know the diatonic triads of the C scale." This may very well be true, but this discussion is to make sure you know how to build and play them ON THE GUITAR. Here is another example:

Starting from this chord: C   You would get the following chord scale:

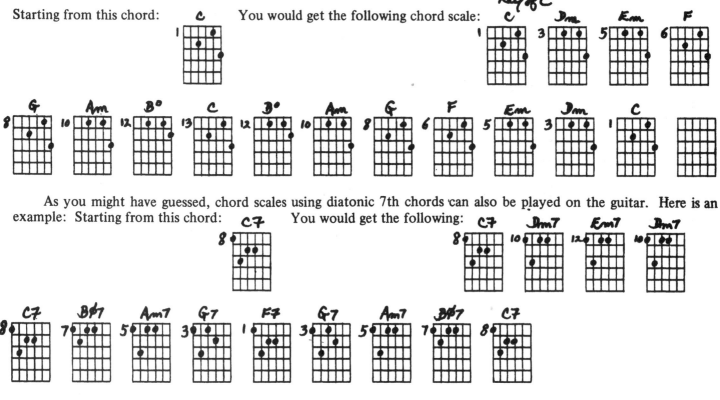

As you might have guessed, chord scales using diatonic 7th chords can also be played on the guitar. Here is an example: Starting from this chord: C7   You would get the following:

The principle is the same as that described above for triads, that is, you just move all the notes in the C7 up to the next notes in the C major scale, thereby creating the other chords.

Now try the following:

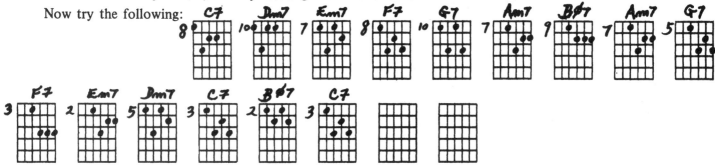

This chord scale utilizes a technique that will be referred to as STRING TRANSFERENCE. Notice that this technique enables you to play a longer chord scale. The secret of being able to utilize this technique lies in the following guidelines:

higher   lower

1. To find the same chord voicing on the next higher group of strings, move all the notes in the chord over to the next higher group of strings; retain the same visual shape unless any note has landed on the 2nd string, in which case you move the note up one fret; now move the whole chord down five frets (or up seven if you want to hear the same chord an octave higher). Now that you're probably totally lost (seriously, if you are, read the directions slowly once more); here is an example:

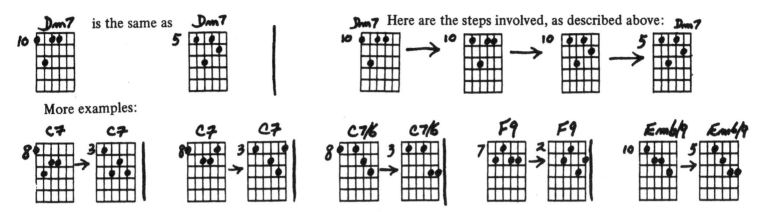

More examples:

2. To find the same chord voicing on the next <u>lower</u> group of strings, move all the notes in the chord over to the next lower group of strings; retain the same visual picture unless any note has landed on the <u>3rd string</u>, in which case you move this note <u>down</u> one fret; now move the whole chord up five frets (or down seven if you want to hear the same chord an octave lower). Examples:

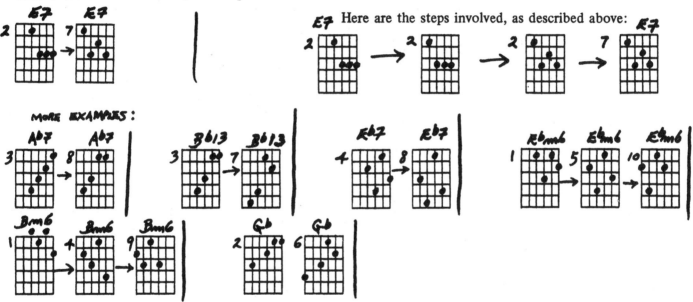

MORE EXAMPLES:

The string transference principle can be helpful in situations where you start to "run out of room". For instance, while the following is theoretically possible:

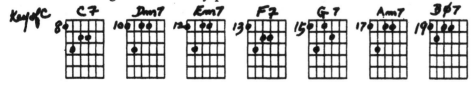

it is not that easy to play the chords on such high frets (also, the <u>sound</u> is weaker up there on the lower strings).

19

But using the string transference principle, you might play any of the following instead:

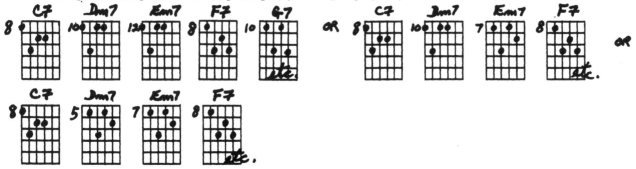

Naturally, all of the information discussed in this section can be applied to any and all keys. Examples: Key of G

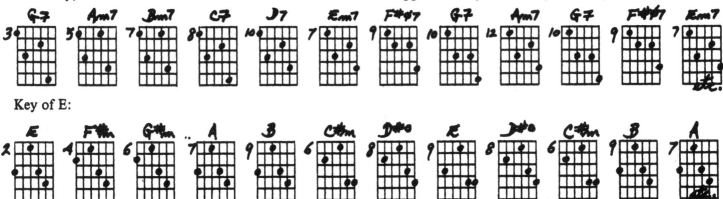

Key of E:

Also, the principles apply to minor scales and keys, but this will be covered later.

A knowledge of chord scales will prove to be most valuable for the serious guitarist; many, many ideas spring from such knowledge.

PRACTICE MATERIAL:

The following is a list of chord forms to start your chord scales from; the forms that would be derived from the string transference method are grouped together (if this is not clear, it will be when you practice building the chord scales from all the forms). The forms are given in the key of E, but you should practice them in all keys eventually.

FORMS FOR DIATONIC CHORD SCALES IN MAJOR KEYS

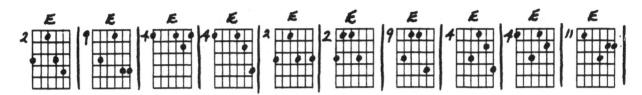

You will notice that these are 1st inversions; there is a certain magic in 1st inversion chord scales that seems to have drawn composers and players to use them more frequently than their root position or 2nd inversion brothers, but this is only true as far as 4-note triads go, not 3-note triads or 7th chords.

One more point that should be mentioned here — these chord scales will be more fun and will sound more interesting if you decorate them. By decoration, I mean "breaking them up" in certain ways such as: 1) delaying notes.

Examples:

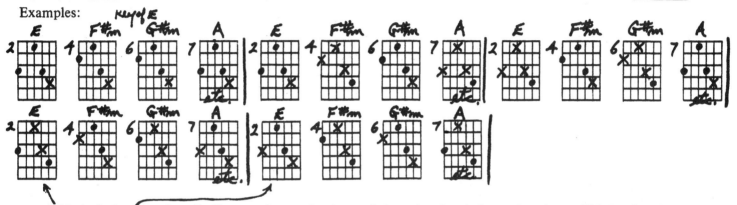

This technique involves finding two interesting intervals in a chord and alternating them. This is what George Van Eps calls the "team concept". Actually, I think George refers to it as this only if separate "teams" of fingers are used in the left hand. For instance, getting two notes with one finger would not be applying the "team" concept.

2) Using moving lines built from other diatonic scale tones.

Examples:

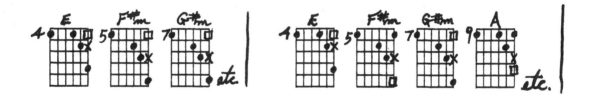

Moving lines are more easily physically played when working with 3-note triads. Here are some more chord forms (this time — 3 note triads) for chord scales and following them, a few more examples illustrating the moving line concept.

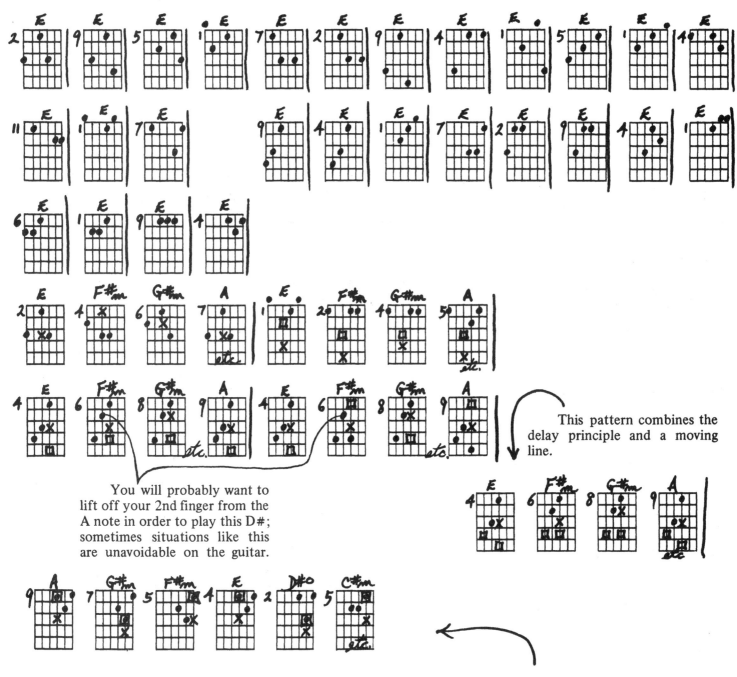

You will probably want to lift off your 2nd finger from the A note in order to play this D#; sometimes situations like this are unavoidable on the guitar.

This pattern combines the delay principle and a moving line.

Notice that the moving effect is transferred to different voices alternately in this example. Also notice that the pattern starts on IV, not I; patterns using chord scales can start on <u>any</u> degree of a scale, according to taste; experiment.

An upcoming book will list many patterns such as these and also many more elaborate ones, but you might enjoy making up some of your own for now. Even just using the delay concept (which is pretty easy to work with once you are used to it), you will come up with lots of sounds.

7th CHORD DIATONIC FORMS
(MAJOR KEY)

Try building diatonic 7th chords from the following forms:

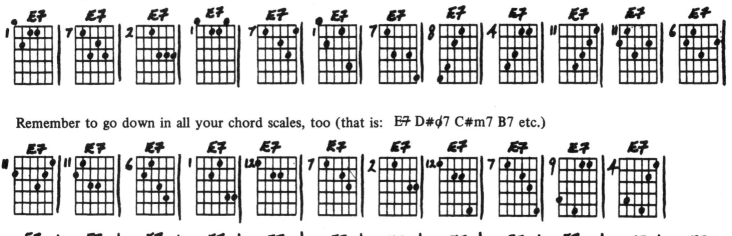

Remember to go down in all your chord scales, too (that is: E7 D#⌀7 C#m7 B7 etc.)

Examples of some decoration:

Breaking these chords up softens the dissonance.

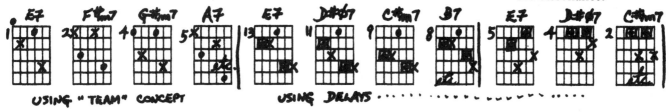

USING "TEAM" CONCEPT   USING DELAYS · · · · · · · · · · · · · · ·

SWR and SWB PROGRESSIONS

This section will deal with two types of progressions:

1. PROGRESSIONS BUILT FROM SCALEWISE ROOT MOVEMENTS (Major Key) (will be abbreviated: SWR)

    Another name for these progressions might be "Progressions derived from diatonic chord scales". Analyze the examples given and you will see why.

2. PROGRESSIONS BUILT FROM SCALEWISE BASS LINES (Major Key) (will be abbreviated: SWB)

    Many pieces of music have been written using these kinds of sounds and you will probably find them to be very attractive. The logic behind them will be clear if you understand your fundamentals of music theory concerning <u>inversions</u>. If you don't, enjoy them anyway, but if you want to construct similar variations, you may have to get your music theory act together.

    Also, Volume 2 will go into this subject of "Bass Progressions" very thoroughly. The few brief examples presented here are just "teasers".

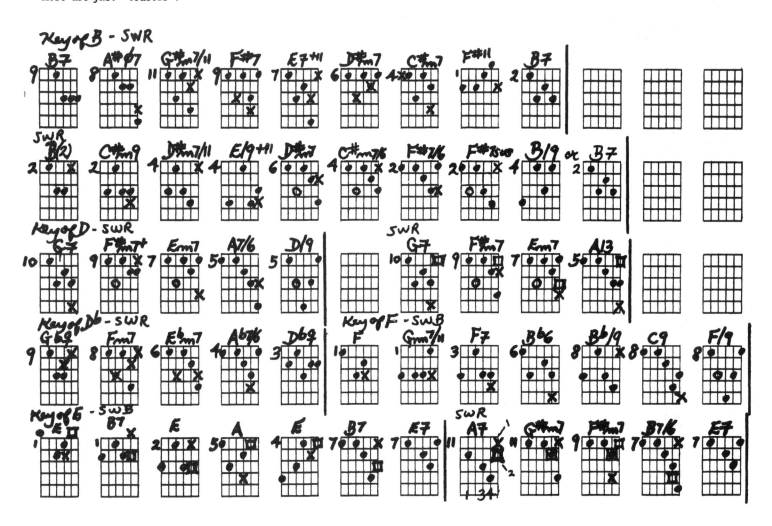

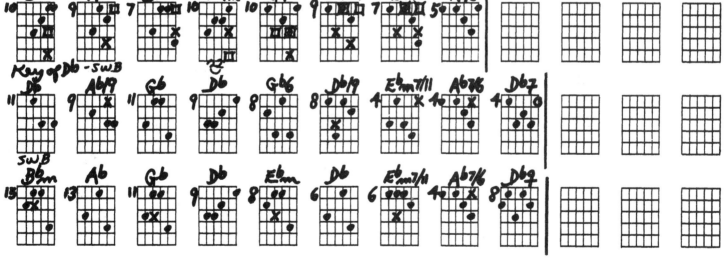

Key of E - SWR

Key of Ab - SWB and SWR

Key of G - SWB

Key of Gb - SWB

NOTICE THAT A I or I I PROGRESSION IS TACKED ON THE END OF THESE PROGRESSIONS. THIS IS COMMONLY DONE TO GIVE THE PHRASES A SENSE OF COMPLETENESS.

Key of D - SWB and SWR

Key of Db - SWB

SWB

I vi ii V (and iii vi ii V)

Another important diatonic harmonic formula is I vi ii V (and the closely related iii vi ii V). This progression has been used as much as probably any other in the history of music. It is especially common to find this progression used as an "opener", meaning the first progression in a song or piece.

You will probably wonder why so many examples of this progression are given ("Look Mabel, this guy Greene's gone crazy — more than twenty pages on the same progression.").

Mainly to show just what can be done with a simple harmonic formula, and also for the purpose of exploring the entire fingerboard from many different angles. All I ask is that you give each example a fair shake, meaning: play each one at least a couple of times with a reasonable amount of continuity and smoothness before making any value judgment about its worthiness. As mentioned earlier, you may run into physical difficulties at first which will prevent you from being able to hear the intended sound of some progressions. In these cases, continued practice of the examples which pose the problems will help you in another way: the progressions then become your friends as far as developing the necessary manual dexterity and coordination which are essential to coping with this difficult instrument.

Remember to pay close attention to the left hand fingering where it is indicated.

You may be curious as to how the many variations on a given harmonic formula are organized. Mainly by melodies (melody here refers to the highest pitch in the chords in almost all cases) starting from different forms (chord shapes). While playing through the examples in order, you will become aware of this. Remember, they are meant to be played in order.

One more thing: You should always try resolving the V to I. Some of the examples will give you ideas on how to do this, especially in the first few pages, but after this, you're on your own. (Volume 2 will have complete charts on the resolution of V to I.)

All examples are given in the keys of C or E at first, later in various keys. This is done to avoid monotony which can creep in if you stay in one key too long. In fact, if anything in music ever sounds monotonous to you, changing the key can be like a breath of fresh air. Try it and see. Say you know a song in the key of G. Changing it to E or B will make a lot of difference. ("Yeah," you're saying, "I won't be able to play it any more.") Seriously, do try changing keys on any of these if you get bored and, as mentioned before, naturally, you should transpose, at least your favorites, to all keys if possible.

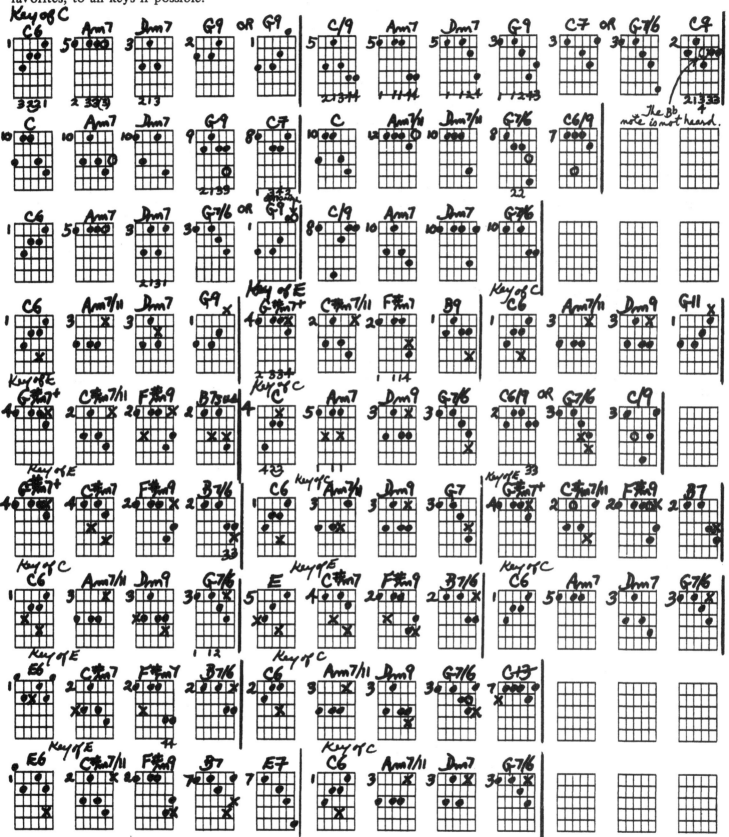

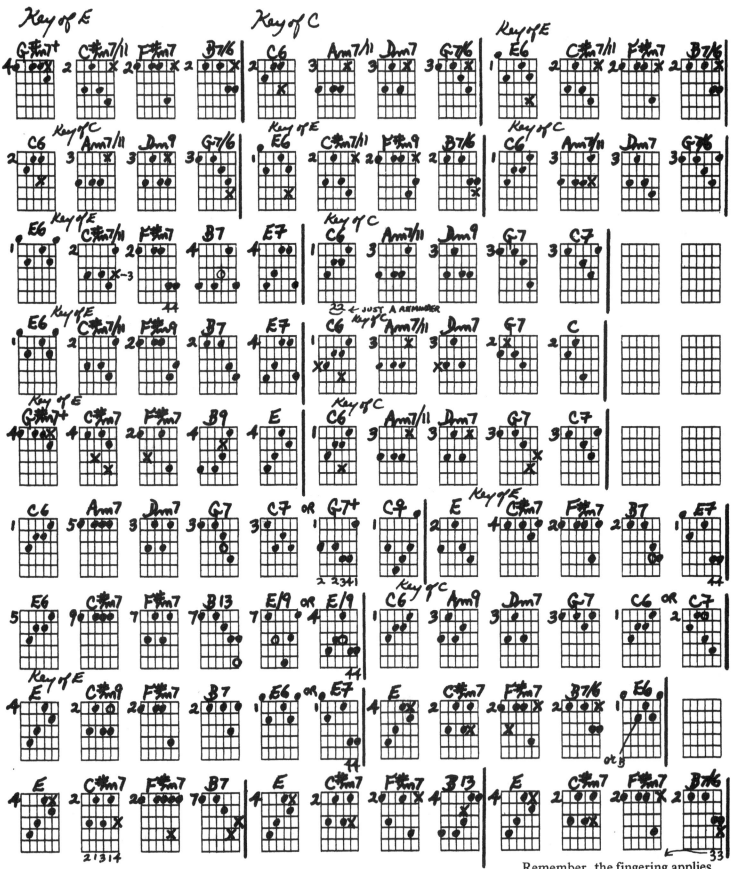

Remember, the fingering applies
to the ●, not the × (unless
otherwise indicated).

28

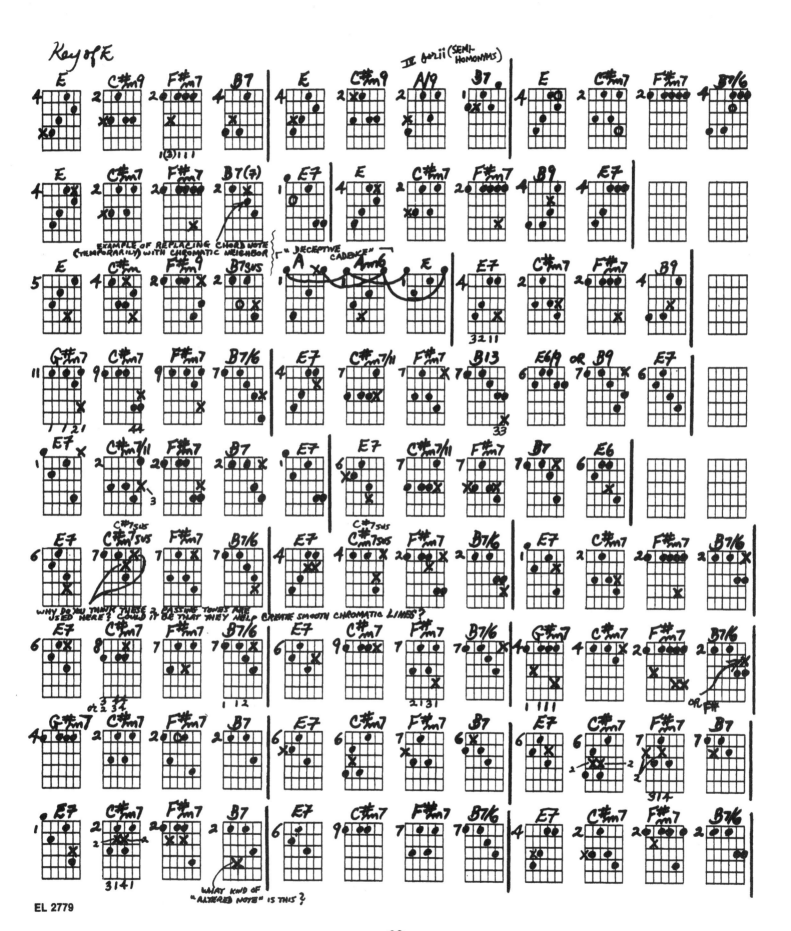

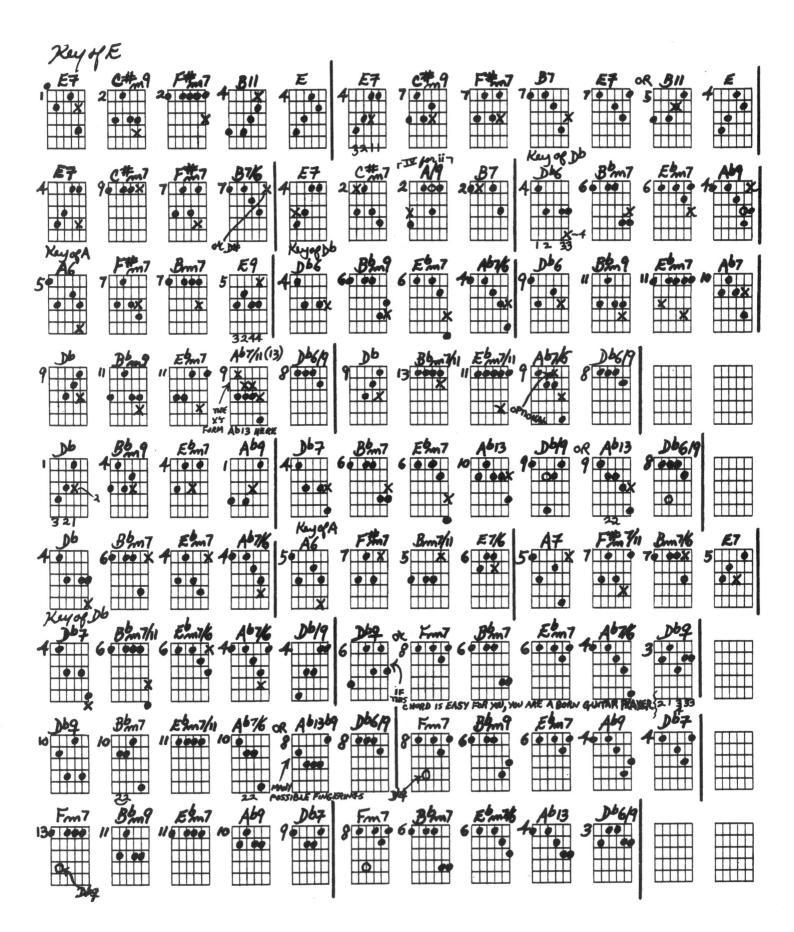

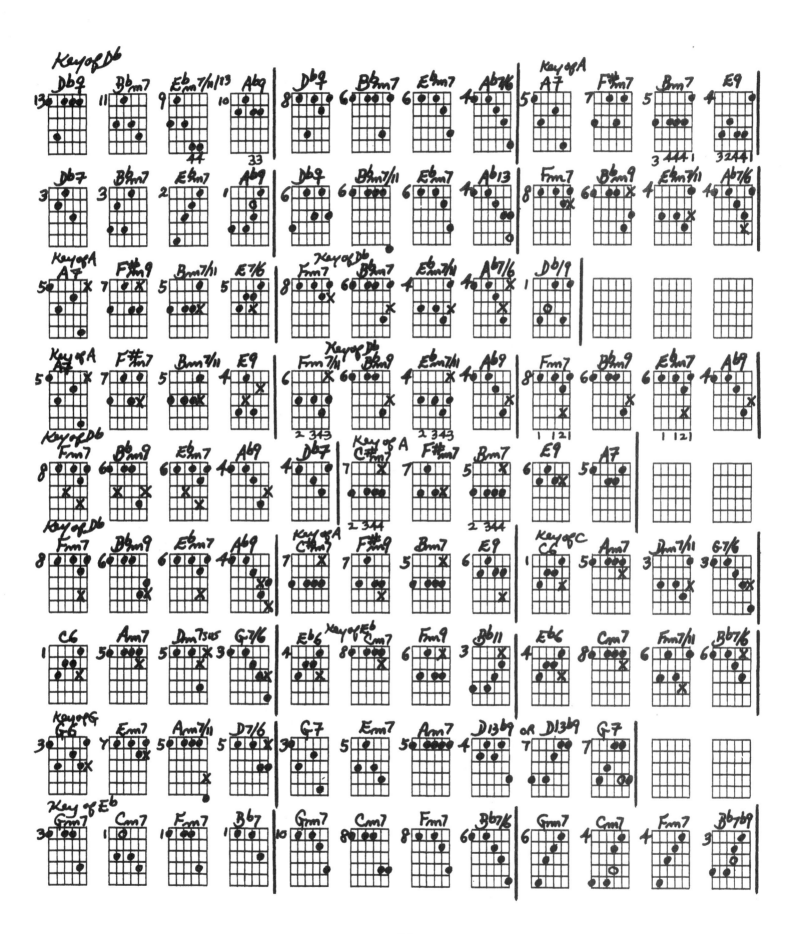

31

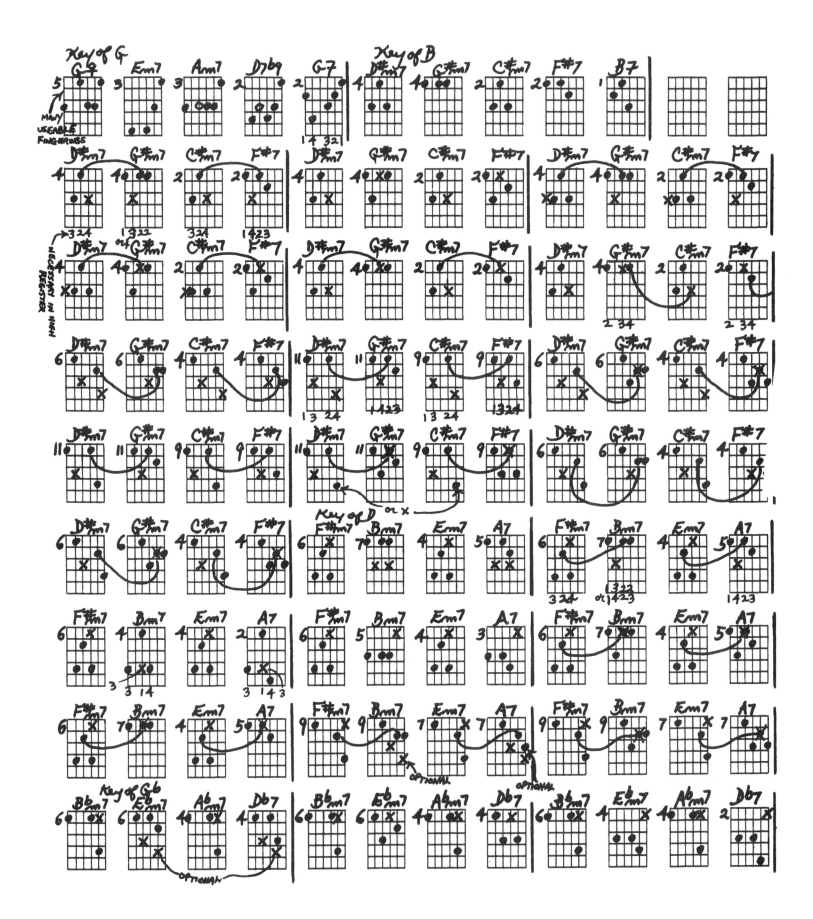

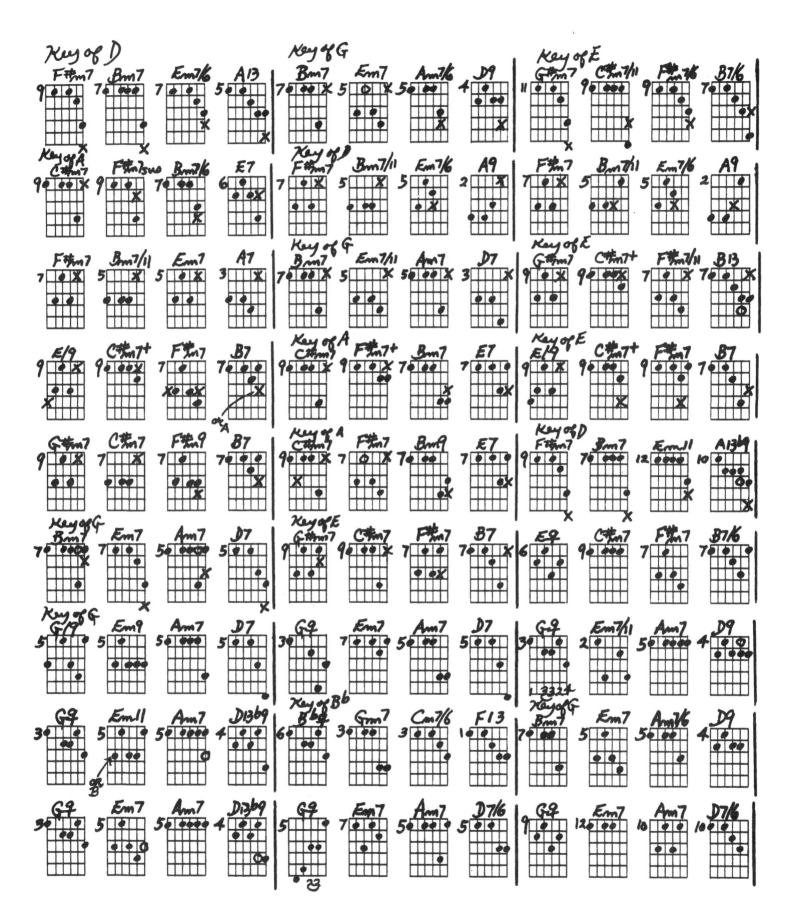

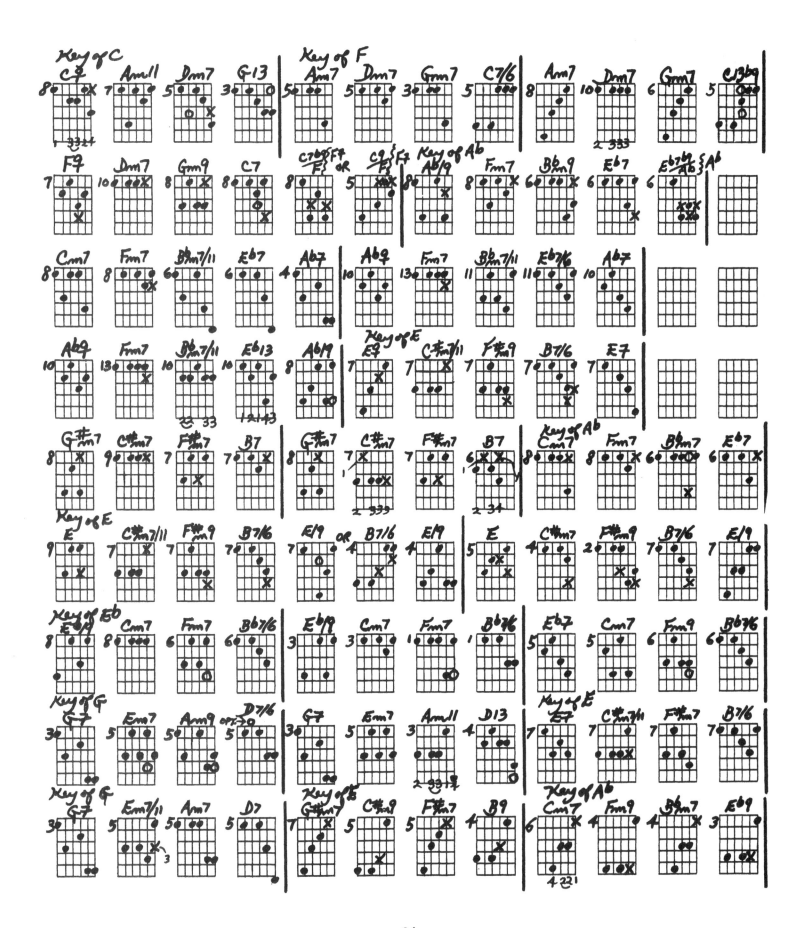

34

35

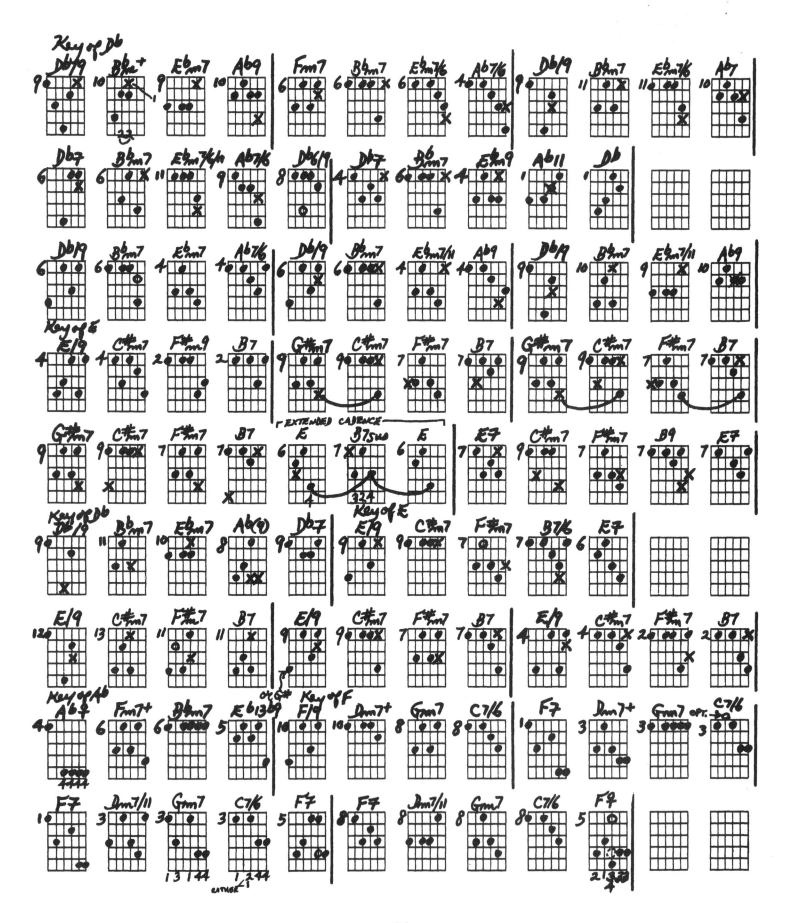

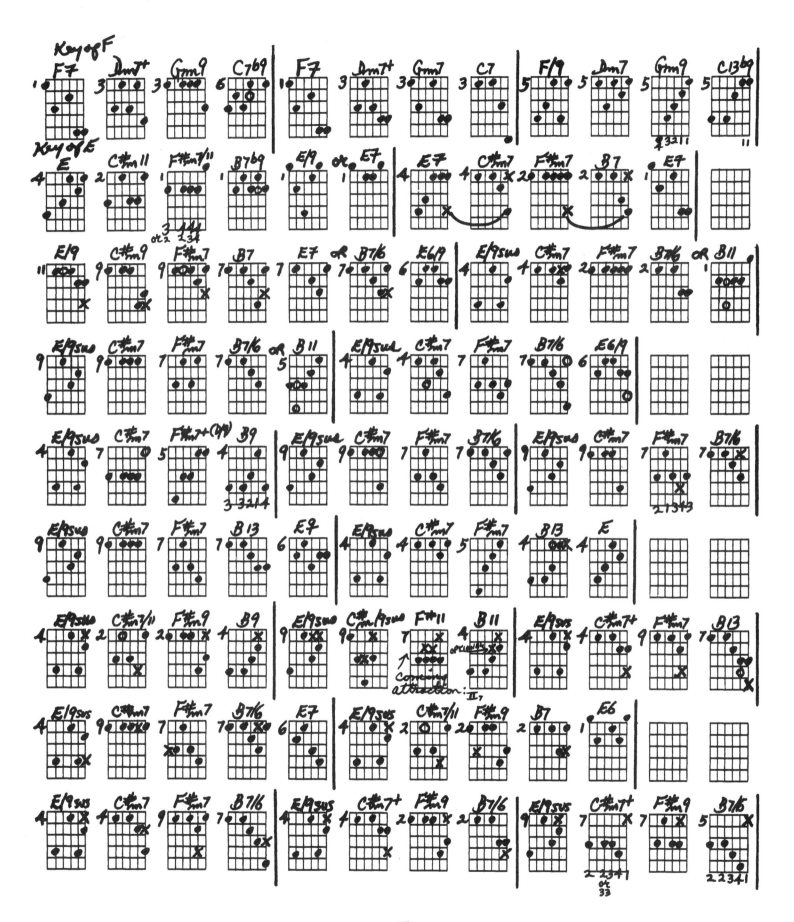

37

38

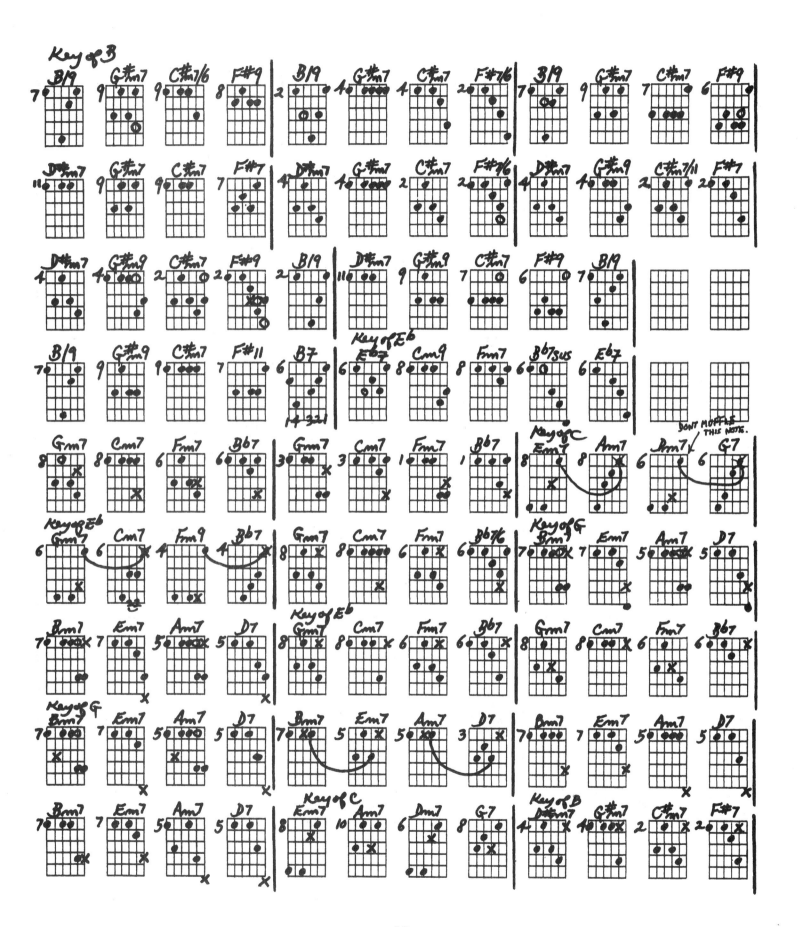

39

40

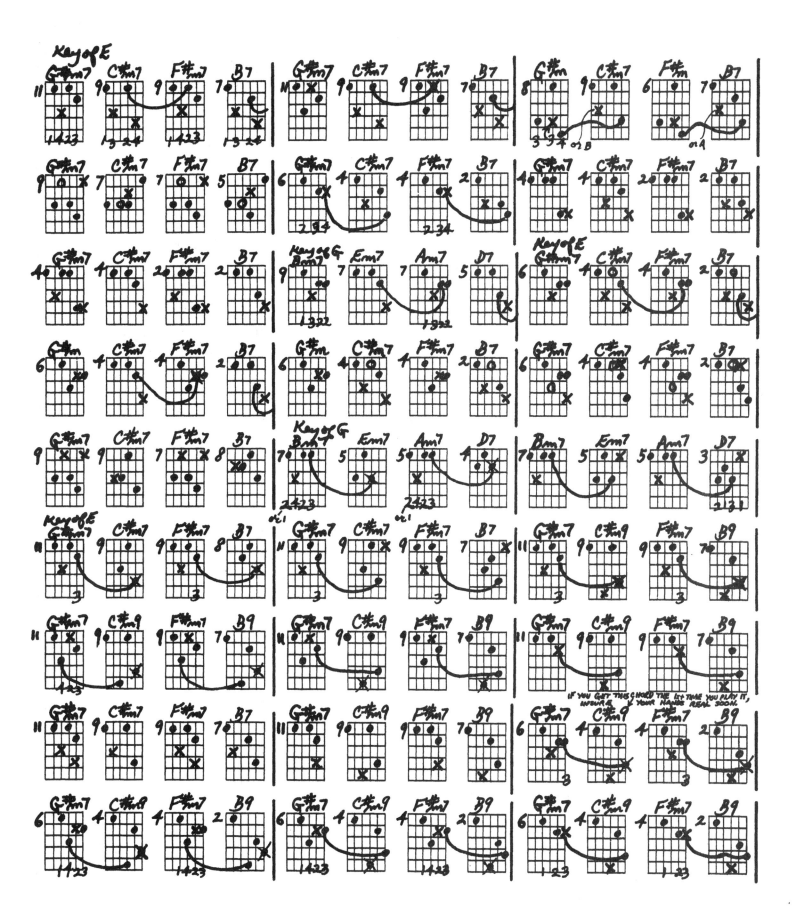

41

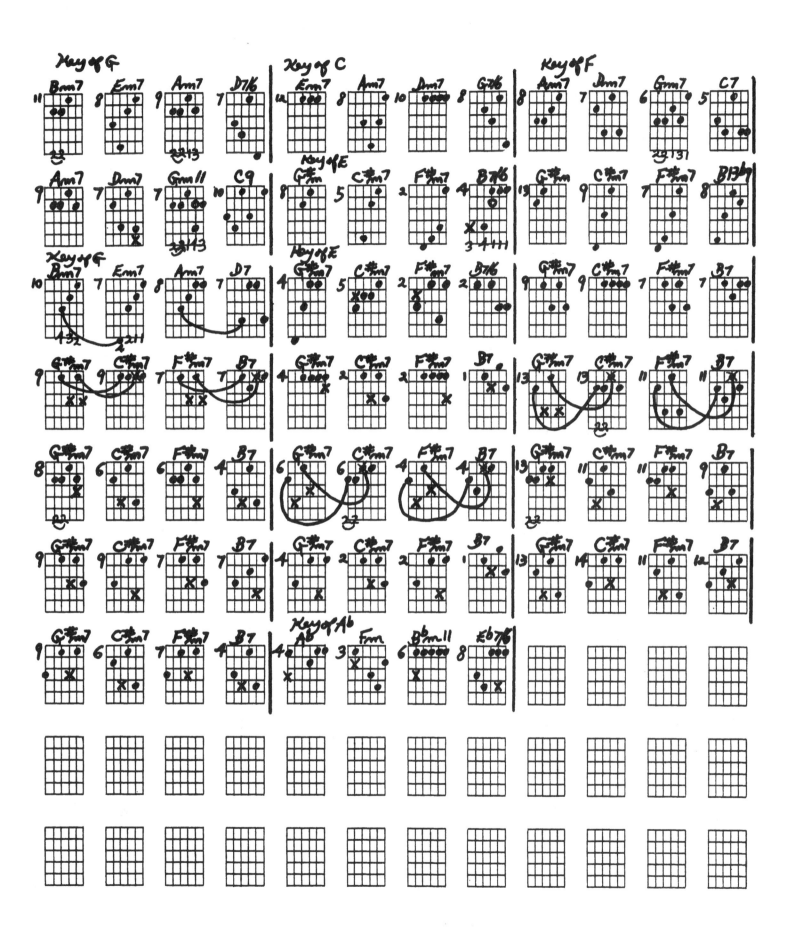

LONGER I vi ii V's and iii vi ii V's

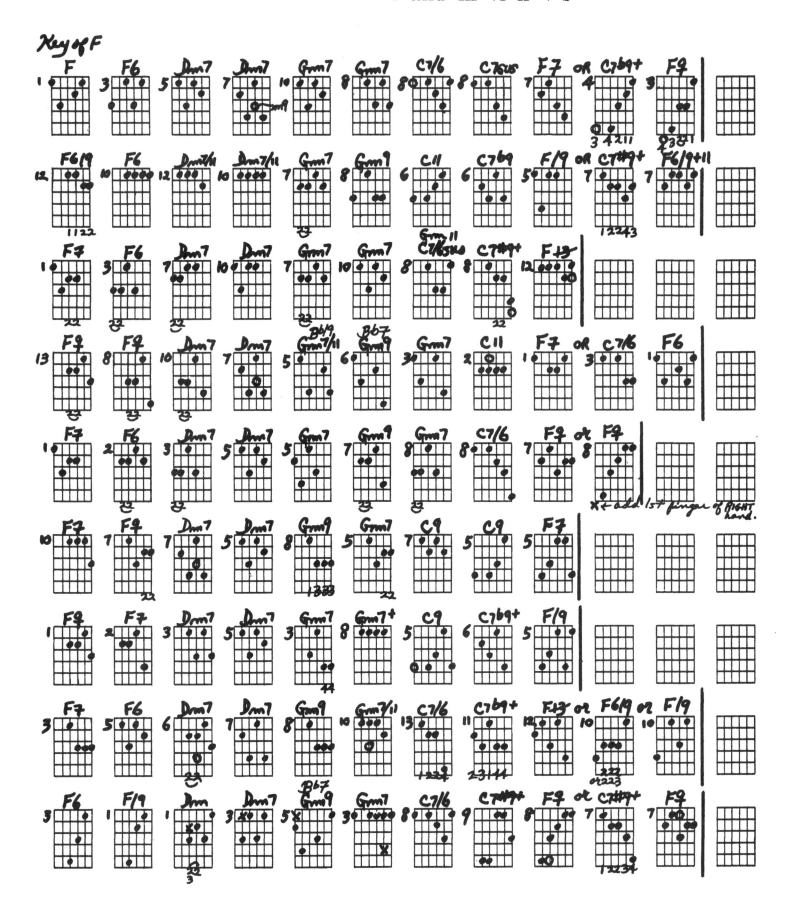

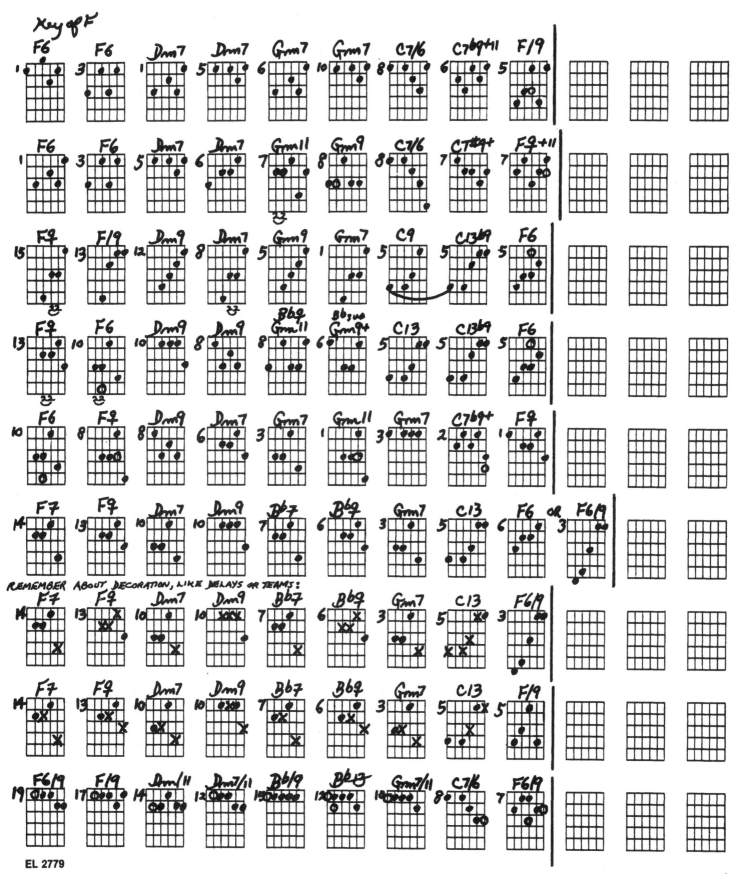

REMEMBER ABOUT DECORATION, LIKE DELAYS OR TEAMS:

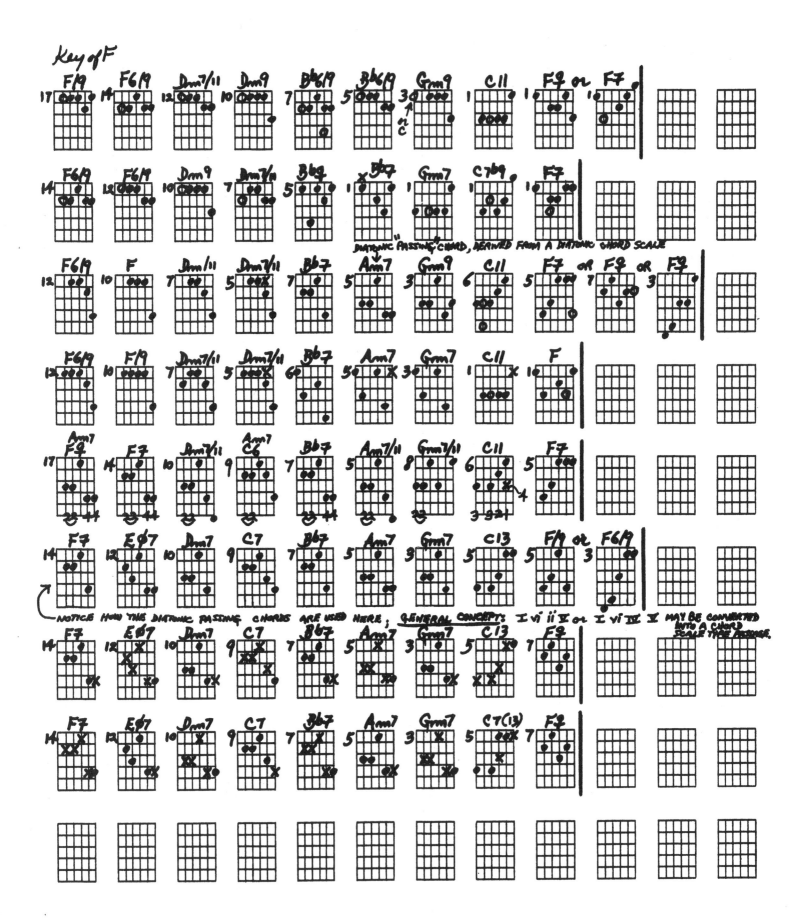

Key of F

46

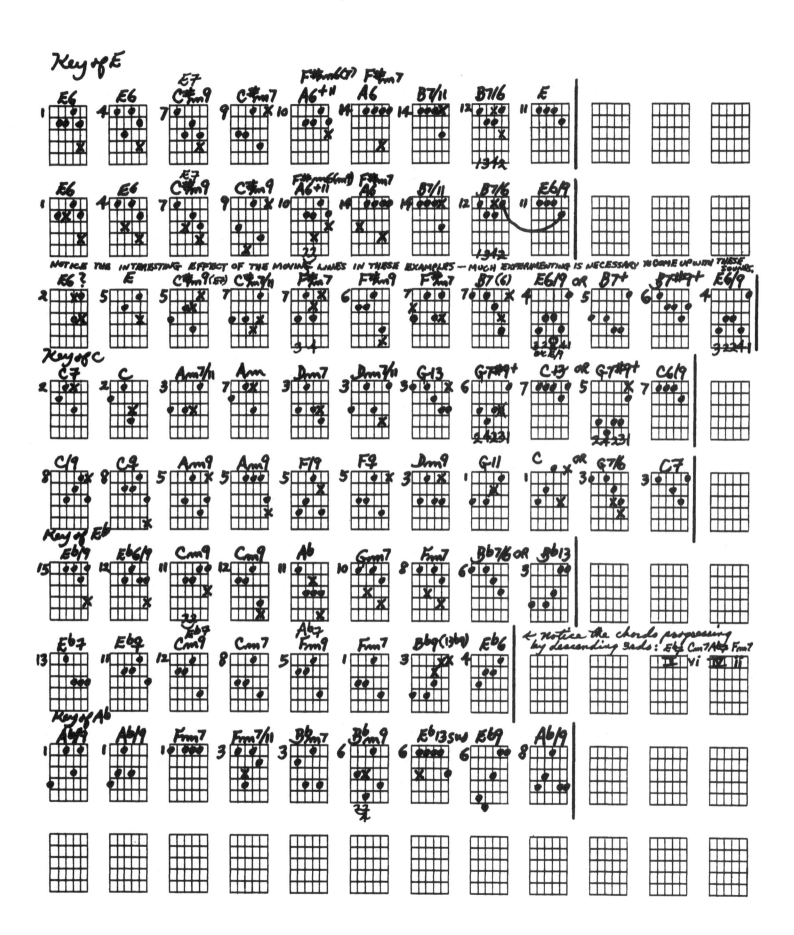

REPEATED I vi ii V's and iii vi ii V's

These sounds can tend to get monotonous if played as given, but later you will be able to use portions (rather than the whole) effectively.

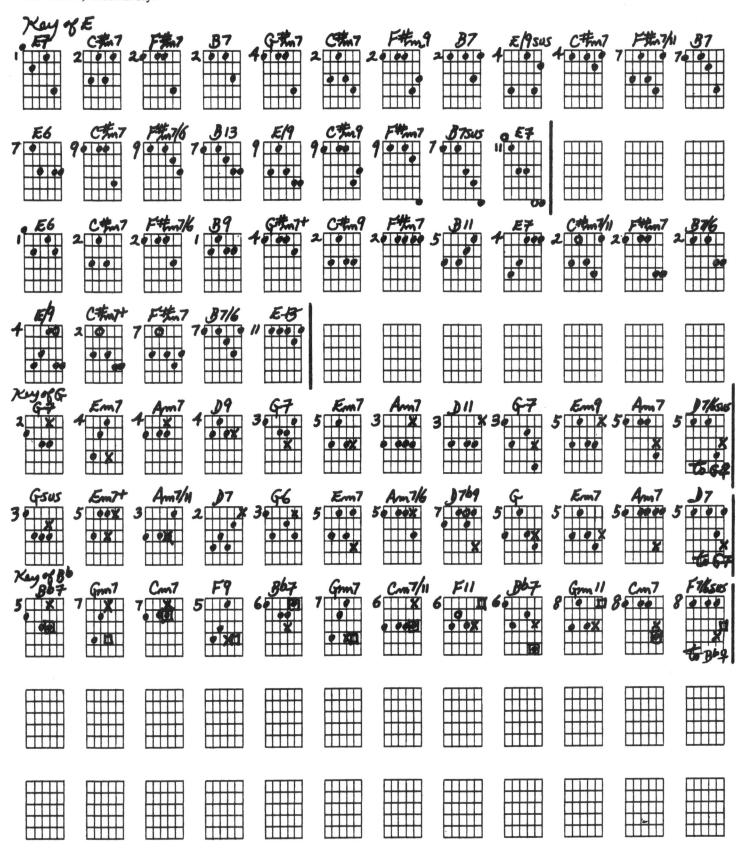

THE DIATONIC CYCLE OF 4THS IN MAJOR KEYS

The harmonic formula I IV vii° iii vi ii V I IV vii° iii vi etc. has been very popular for a long time. It is often referred to as the CYCLE OF 4ths (or 5ths) meaning each chord root is a 4th higher (or 5th lower) than the previous chord root. Example: In the key of C, using 7th chords, the diatonic cycle of 4ths is C7 F7 Bm7♭5 Em7 Am7 Dm7 G7 C7 F7 etc.   I   IV   vii°   iii   vi   ii
V I IV

Looking at the root names of the chords, you will see that F is a 4th above C, B is a 4th (#4th) above F, E is a 4th above B, and so on.

Notice that iii vi ii V, with which you are already familiar, is contained in the cycle of 4ths. Also you should know that it is common for the cycle to begin on other chords than the I; for instance, you might encounter the cycle in a song in the following form: IV vii° iii vi ii V I. No matter which chord it starts on, as long as each chord is a 4th higher in the key, it is still the diatonic cycle of 4ths.

Most cycles of 4ths use a SEQUENCE pattern (a sequence is an exact repetition of a musical idea but using <u>different</u> pitches. Example: *Key of C:*

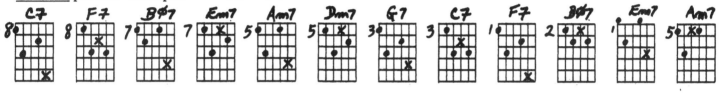

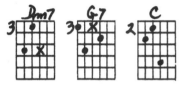

Notice that the sequence pattern used here involves units of <u>two</u> chords: C7 F7, B∅7 Em7, Am7 Dm7, G7 C7, F7 B∅7, etc. (the string transference slightly changed the pattern at the end, but unfortunately the physical limits of the instrument necessitate this type of thing sometimes, if you wish to keep a pattern going a little longer).

One trick to creating a good cycle of 4ths pattern is to get a good connection of the first two chords, and then carry the pattern down. This is where your knowledge of chord scales comes in. **IMPORTANT: A cycle of 4ths pattern as illustrated above, can also be viewed as two chord scales descending, while they alternate with each other.**

Try playing just the first, third and fifth diagrams above; now play just the second, fourth and sixth diagrams. The first, third and fifth diagrams belong to one chord scale and the second, fourth and sixth diagrams belong to another.

Here is another example: *Key of A:*

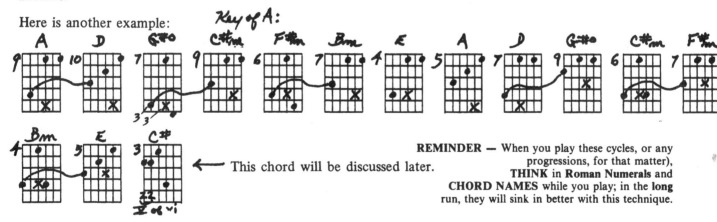

← This chord will be discussed later.

REMINDER — When you play these cycles, or any progressions, for that matter), **THINK** in **Roman Numerals** and **CHORD NAMES** while you play; in the **long** run, they will sink in better with this technique.

49

Again notice that once the initial good connection of I and IV is made, it is just a matter of figuring out the descending chord scales from both chords and alternating them. The fingering on the G#° and F#m chords near the beginning was also changed to make the playing a little easier (don't laugh, in the long run these fingerings will be easier; likewise the fingering on the C#m and Bm near the end).

OK, so how do you find all these good I to IV connections? Well, you can try and find them yourself or you can consult the following list. Only the I and IV chords will be given in this list, but you should make them into cycle of 4th patterns (if you are going to work with them) by figuring out the chord scales, most of which you already know if you have done your homework. Occasionally the IV and vii° chords will be given instead of the I and IV, for the sake of variety. But the procedure of figuring out the cycle by the two alternating chord scales is still the same, whether you start from IV vii° or I IV.

Here is an example of a diat. cycle of 4ths starting from IV:

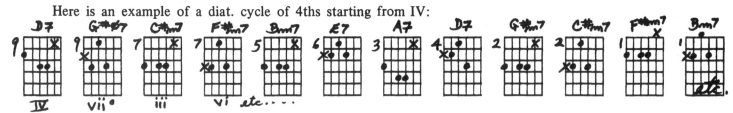

You will see some of your old friends from the iii vi ii V progressions cropping up as you are playing these, which should be helpful in memorizing them. So, it is not as if you are starting from scratch on this subject — you already know many chord scales and some iii vi ii V I patterns, so it is just a question of putting the information together in a slightly different light.

Sometimes you will have to leave a note out of a chord (or change a note), due to the physical problem.

Example: If this chord should occur in a cycle   you might change it to

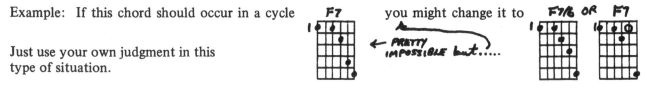

Just use your own judgment in this type of situation.

To really know the whole instrument, you should practice each cycle in all octaves on each string set. For example, if you are given   the first cycle pattern you will come up with will be as follows:

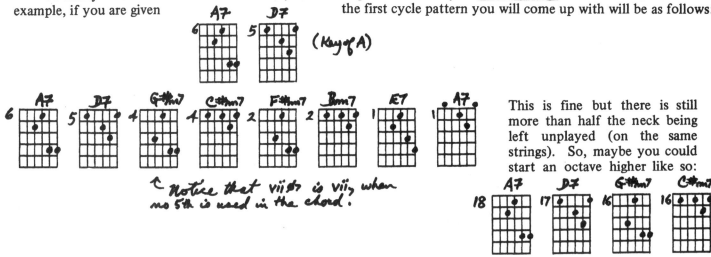

This is fine but there is still more than half the neck being left unplayed (on the same strings). So, maybe you could start an octave higher like so:

Or if you can't play that high on your particular guitar, you could at least start on IV (or some other chord).

50

Some chords (particularly iii7b9 and vii7b9) that you will encounter as part of a few cycles will not sound too great, but the rest of the chords in those cycles will make the whole thing worth checking out anyway.

Be prepared to see some amazing inverse relationships with cycles (nothing to worry about, this will be clear, and you will probably get a kick out of them as well).

Finally, one reminder: The cycle of 4ths is a beautiful harmonic tool, but it can be monotonous if overused, so try combining it eventually, with other ideas. You will be learning more about this in later volumes of this series, as mentioned, but there is no harm in experimenting right away on your own. Even just combining different cycle patterns might be fun for now.

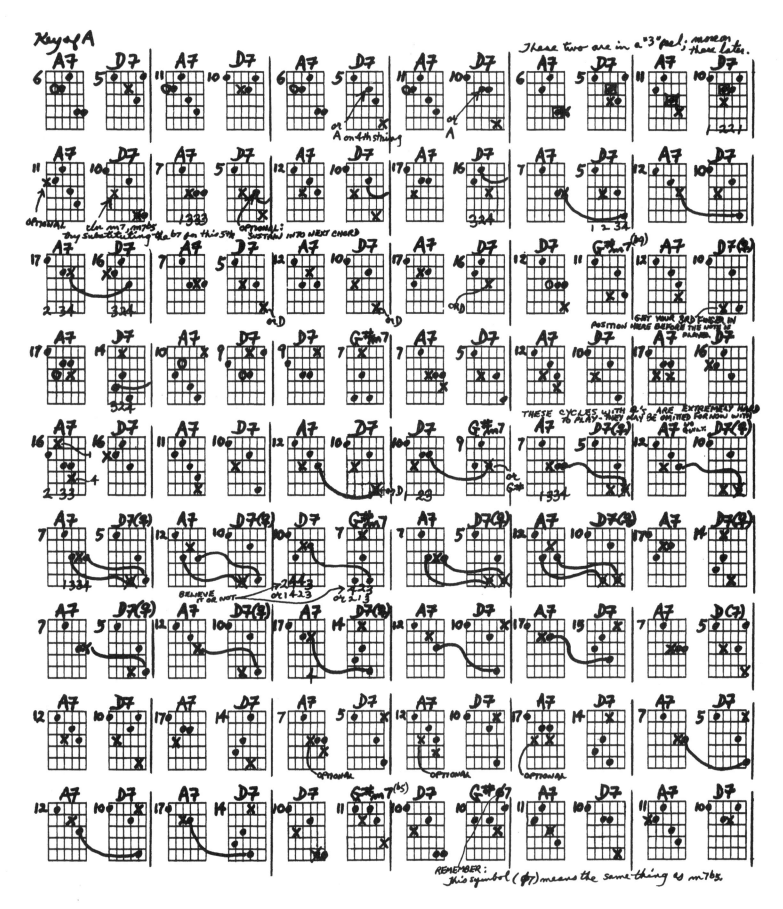

52

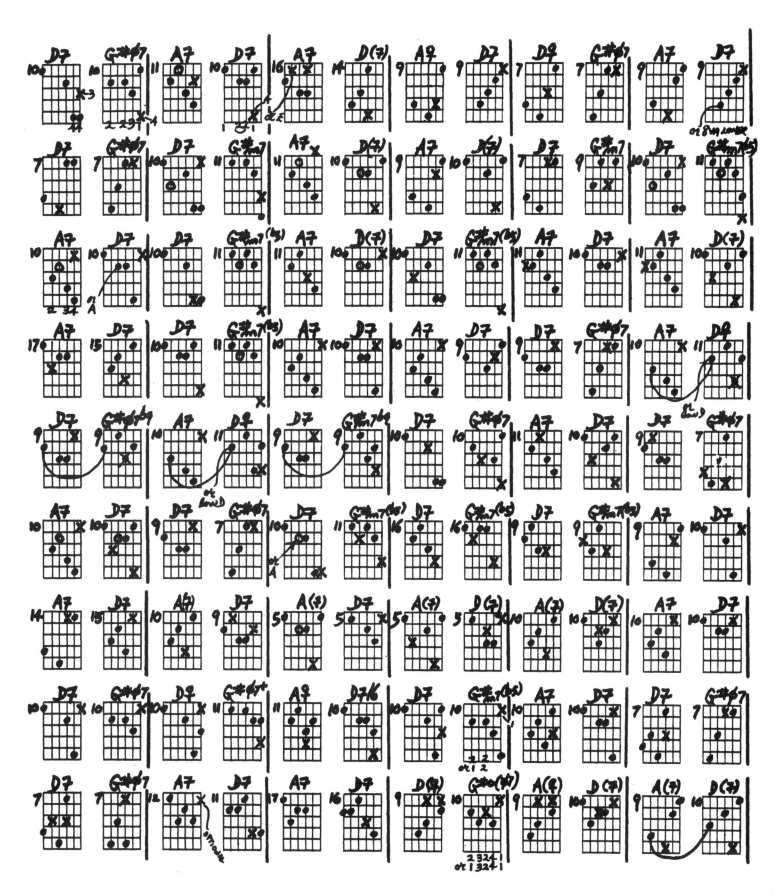

53

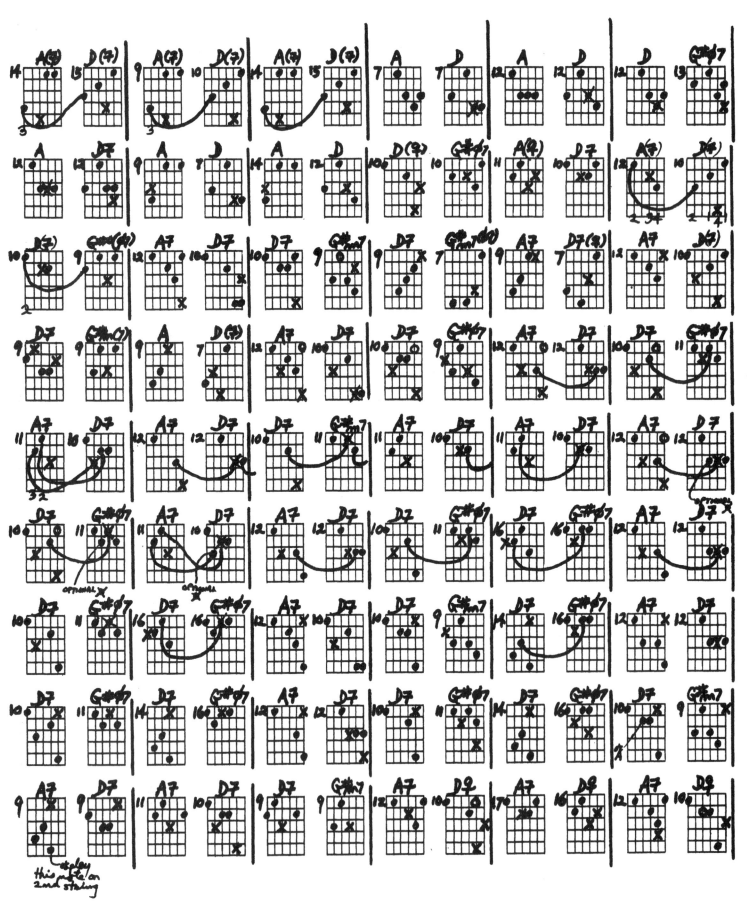

54

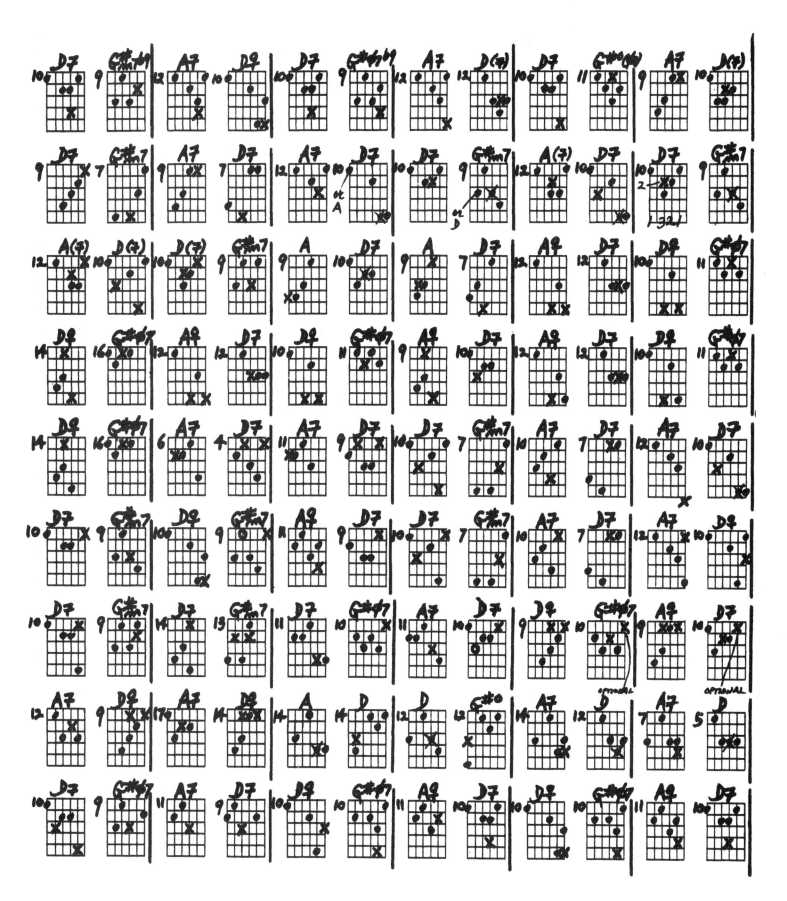

55

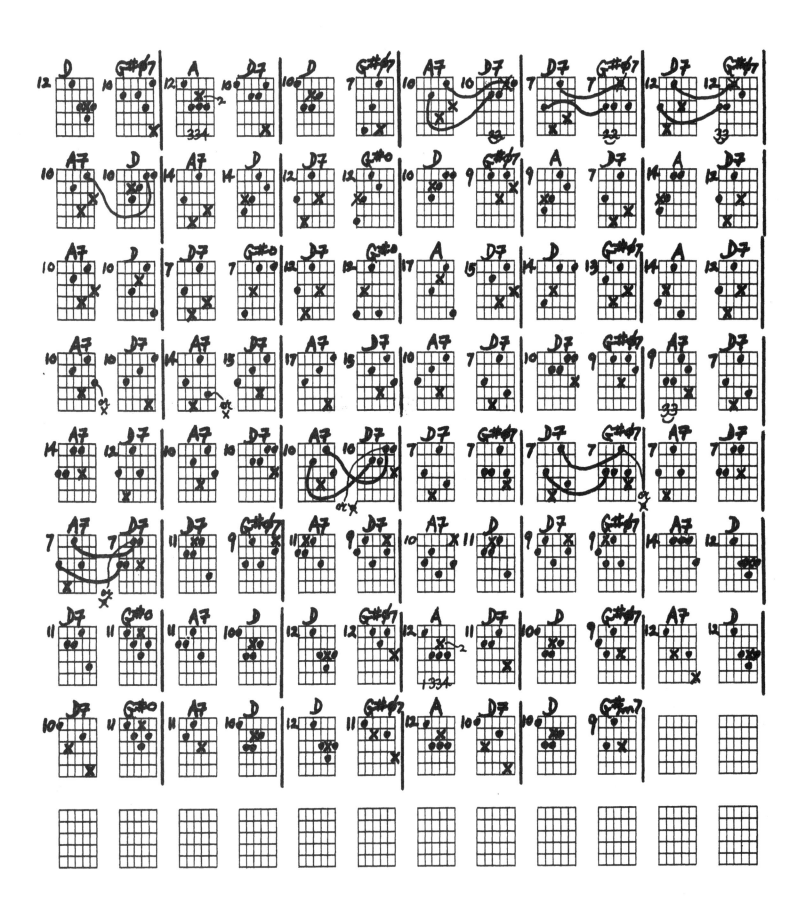

56

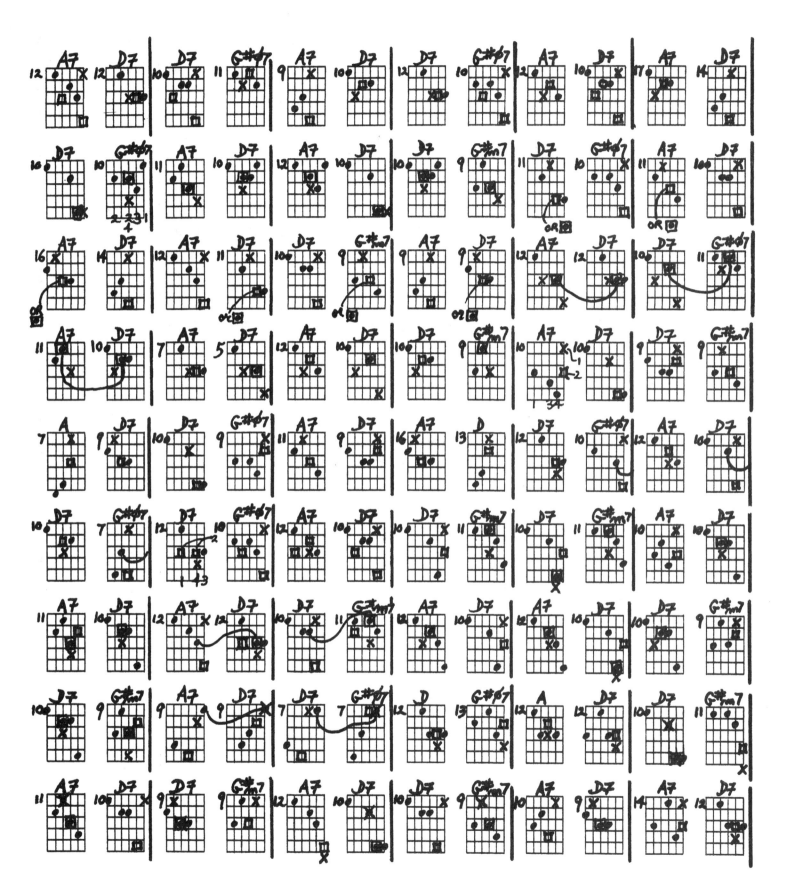

57

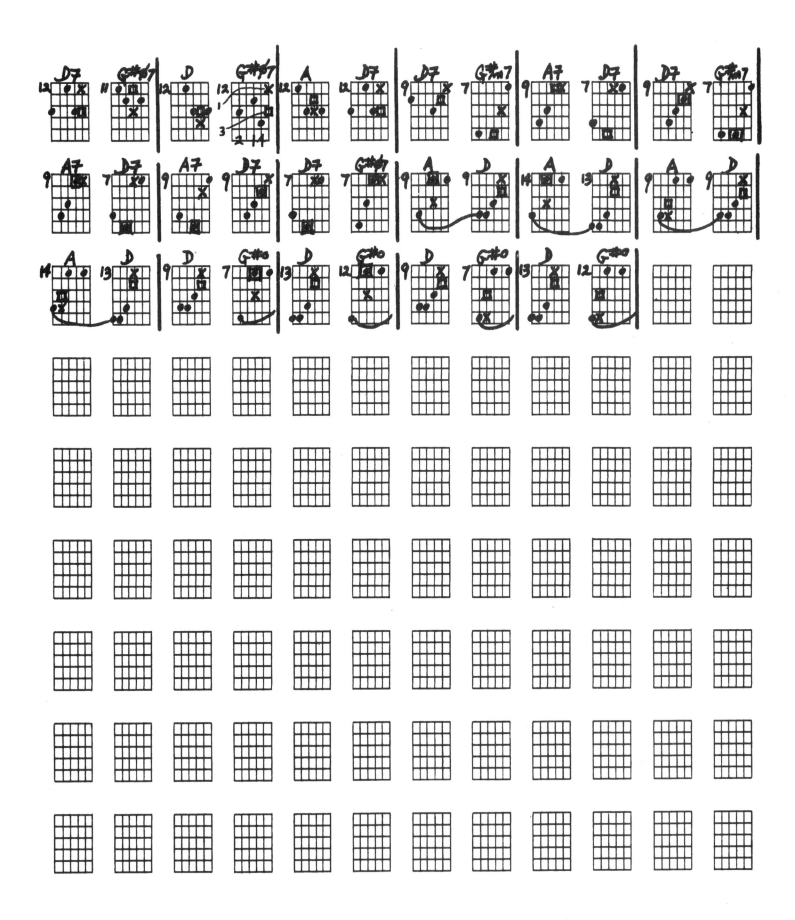

58

PROGRESSIONS USING SUBSTITUTE CHORDS (MAJOR KEY)

iii7 VI7 ii7 V7 (and I7 VI7 ii7 V7)

Many chord progressions in major keys use chords that are not diatonic. You have already seen some examples of ii or V chords that were not diatonic. Example: F#m7+ and B7b9 in the key of E ... the F#m7+ contains a D note and B7b9 contains a C note and, as you know (I hope), both of these notes are non-diatonic to the key of E. Chords such as these are what we will call SUBSTITUTE CHORDS and soon we will work with some new common harmonic formulas that utilize such creatures. But first, one simple, yet very important, concept must be stated: ANY m7 TYPE CHORD MAY BE REPLACED WITH A DOMINANT 7th TYPE CHORD, ACCORDING TO PERSONAL TASTE. This principle is very commonly utilized in almost all kinds of music. For instance, suppose you are playing a song in the key of C, and you see the progression C E7 Am; there is the concept at work — E7 is replacing the normal Em7 (III7 is replacing iii7). If you keep your eyes and ears open, you will start noticing similar applications of the "dominant for minor" principle in much music that you already hear.

Anyway, the first new harmonic formula is going to be iii7 VI7 ii7 V7 where VI7 can be any dominant 7th type chord (7th chord symbols are going to be used from now on, most of the time; to make sure we have our symbols straight, vi7 in C would be Am7 while VI7 would be A7).

Occasionally, I7 will be used for iii7. You will notice that VI7 and V7 commonly use what are usually referred to as ALTERED TONES (namely b5, #5, b9 or #9). In fact, in a iii7 VI7 ii7 V7 progression, these are the norm rather than the exception. Why is this? Because they sound good. And why is this? I tried to work out a simple explanation for this and kept running up against a subject that requires a complex explanation to do it justice, and also depends to some extent on personal taste. So rather than waste your time and mine, it seemed more reasonable to just give many good examples of the progressions, and let you be your own teacher on this subject, if you care to be. Actually, if you are like most players who deal with this subject, you will make and remember your own "rules" as far as what type of colors you prefer on a given degree. Example: You might say to yourself, "7b9+ chords are great on VI7;" this is a "rule" you might remember. Or you might go further and generalize in a similar manner to what was said before: "VI7 sounds good with any altered tone when the VI7 is used in smooth connection with the chords that precede or follow it." (The examples will illustrate the wide range of ground that the term "smooth connection" really covers).

For the curious: There are reasons for most of the musical phenomena enjoyed by the human ear but don't be afraid to admit that some questions as to the "Whys?" may lead to dead-ends or back to the same central question, the one fundamental question underlying all life. For example, let's follow the chain of questions generated by the question, "Why does a 7b9+ chord sound good on VI? (In other words, if we are in the key of C, why does the A7b9+ sound good when used smoothly with other chords?)" Possible answer: Most of the notes are diatonic to the major scale of the key of the I chord. Question: Why does a major scale sound good? Possible answer: Because it is based on the tones of the major chord which is part of Nature's overtone series. Question: Why should Nature base its overtone series on the major triad? Or even more basic, why is there an overtone series in the first place? (If you are not aware of the overtone series, it should prove very interesting for you to check it out.) Possible answer: Apparently for man's enjoyment. Last question: Why?

Although a questioning mind is one of your best friends, and this is in no way meant to deter such a spirit, there are certain things that may have to be accepted on a "that's the way it is" basis, at least for now. Can you answer the question, "Why does man have only five fingers on each hand, instead of six or nine or eleven and a half?" The person who can answer this type of question will probably help us answer our most basic questions about music as well.

The iii7 VI7 ii7 V7 pattern has within itself the potential for many different colors and moods; in this section (as well as others) of the book, you will encounter sounds which were used in different time periods during the history of classical, jazz and popular music. For instance, play the following:

59

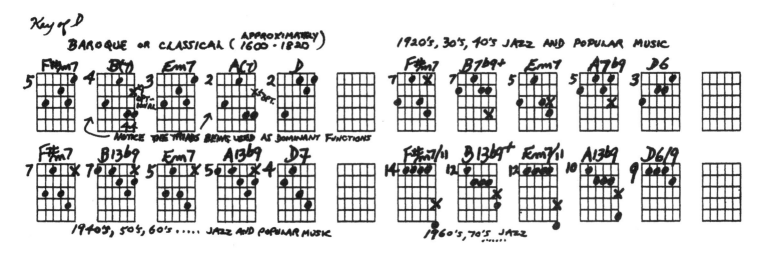

Quite a difference in their colors, right? And yet they are all (still) iii VI ii V's. The differences have to do with the particular VOICINGS and CHORD QUALITIES; you will be encountering all these types of sounds in the progressions to follow.

You will notice a different type of organization in this section . . . all progressions from any given "starting" chord are pretty much grouped together. A good way to memorize your favorites is to first make a list of all the different starting chords given in these iii (I) VI ii V's, and then group your favorites accordingly. (In fact, this technique would be good on the I vi ii V section also.) Remember to resolve the V7's to I's occasionally.

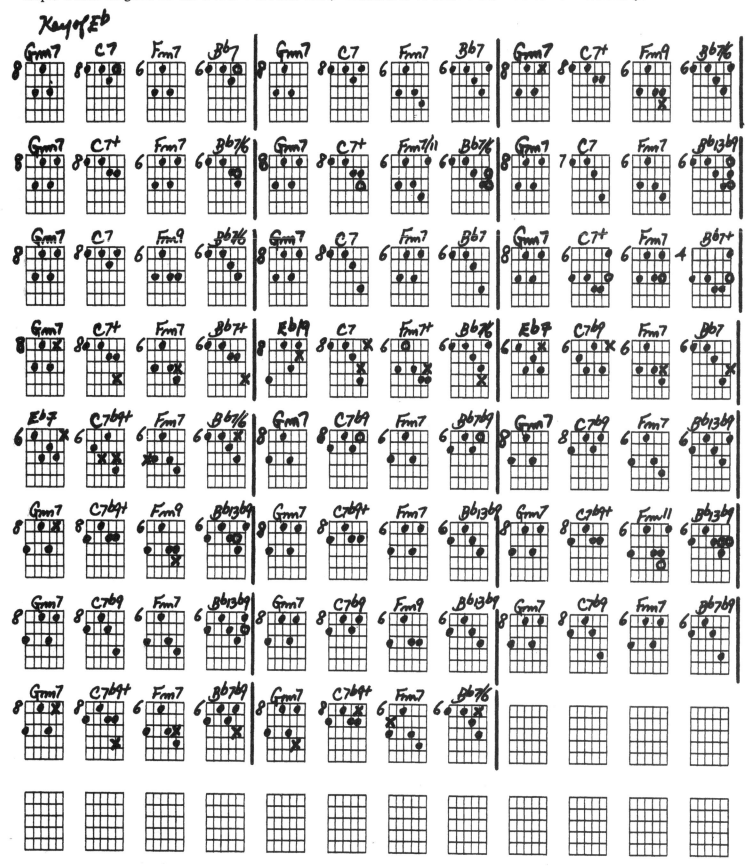

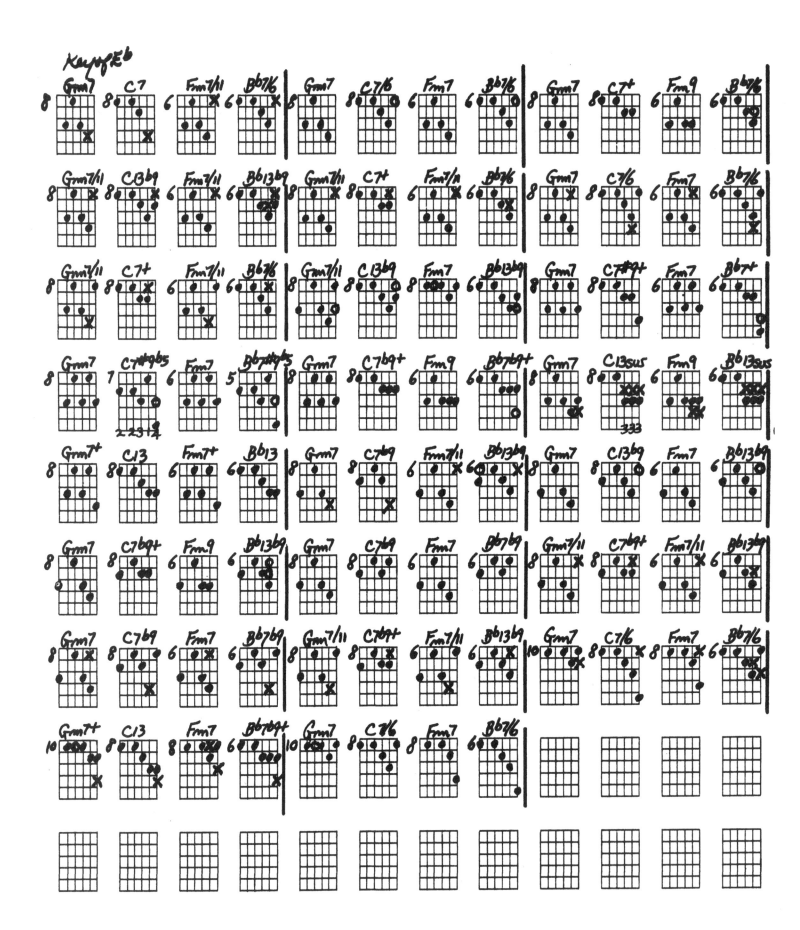

62

63

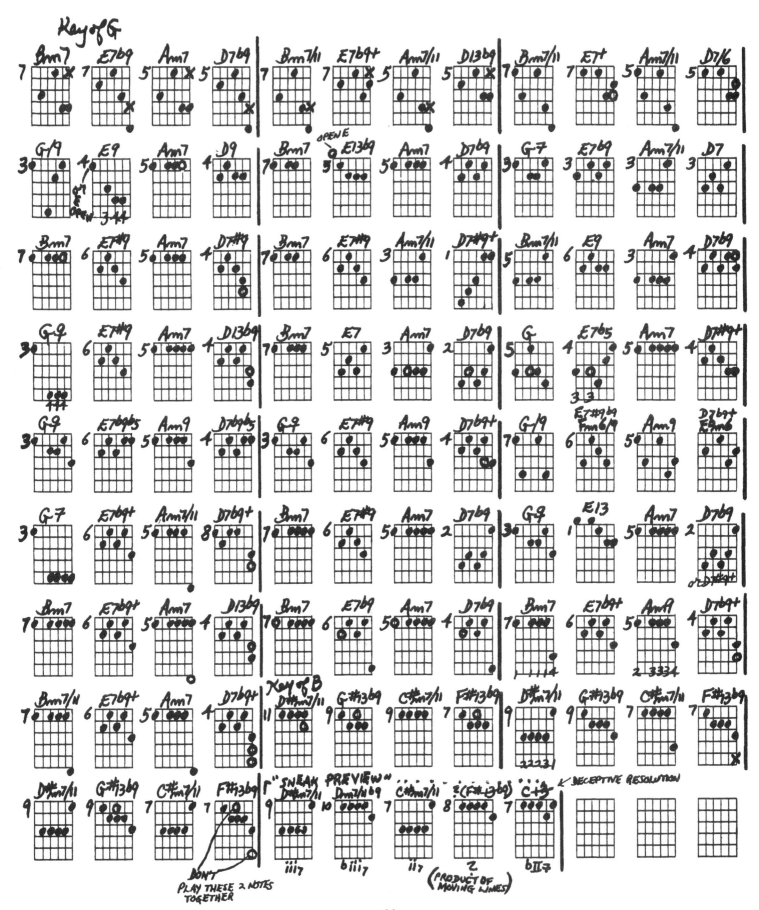

64

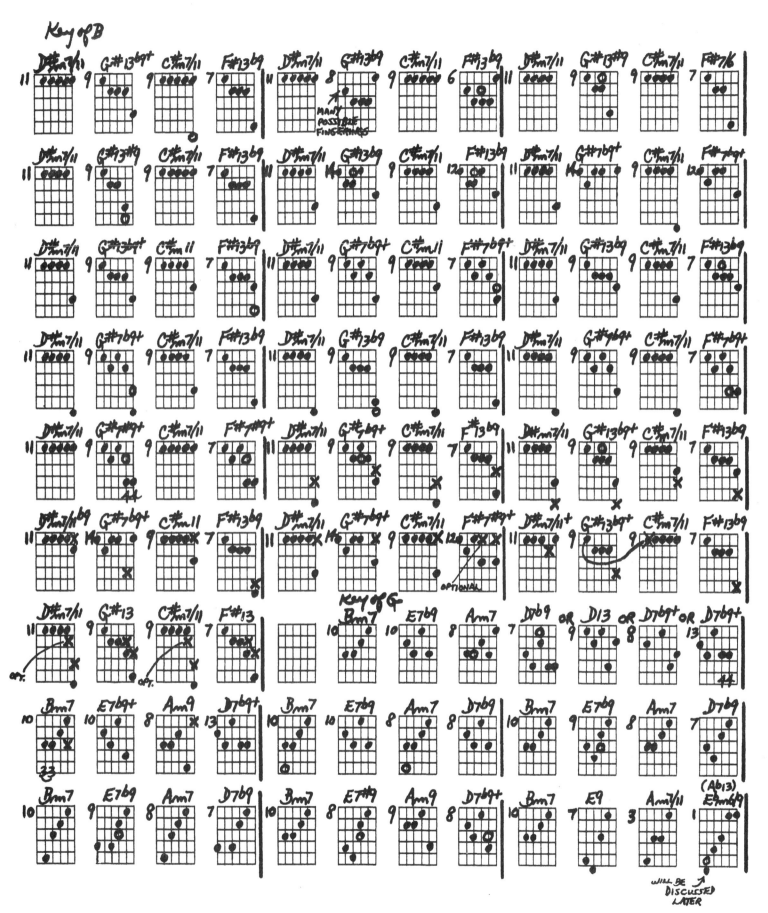

65

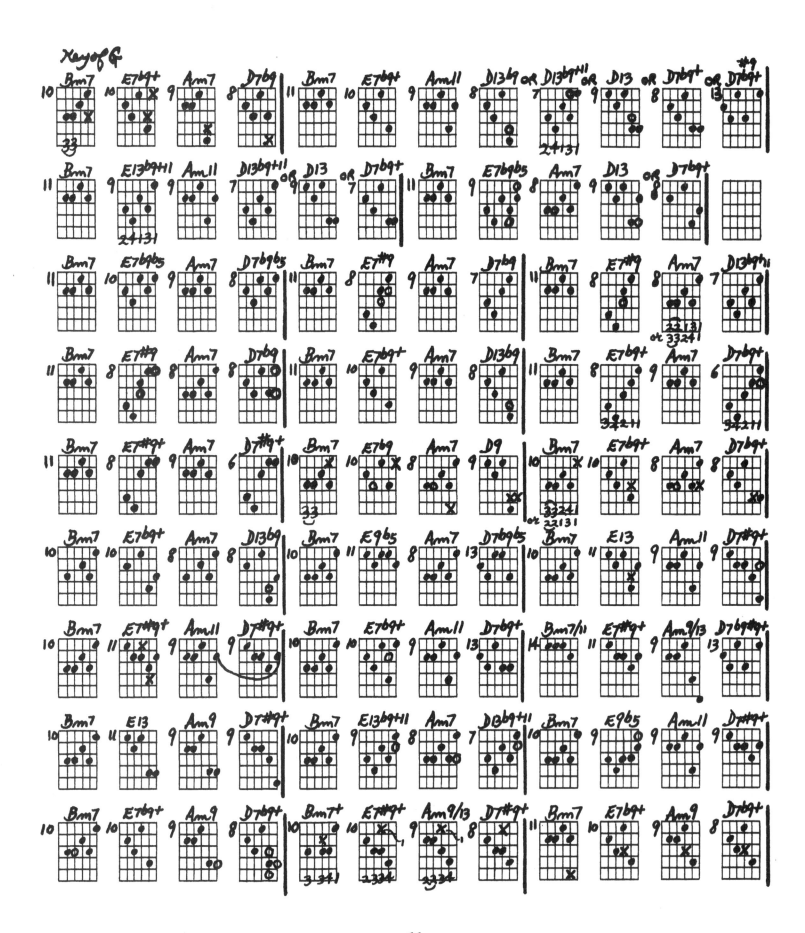

Key of G

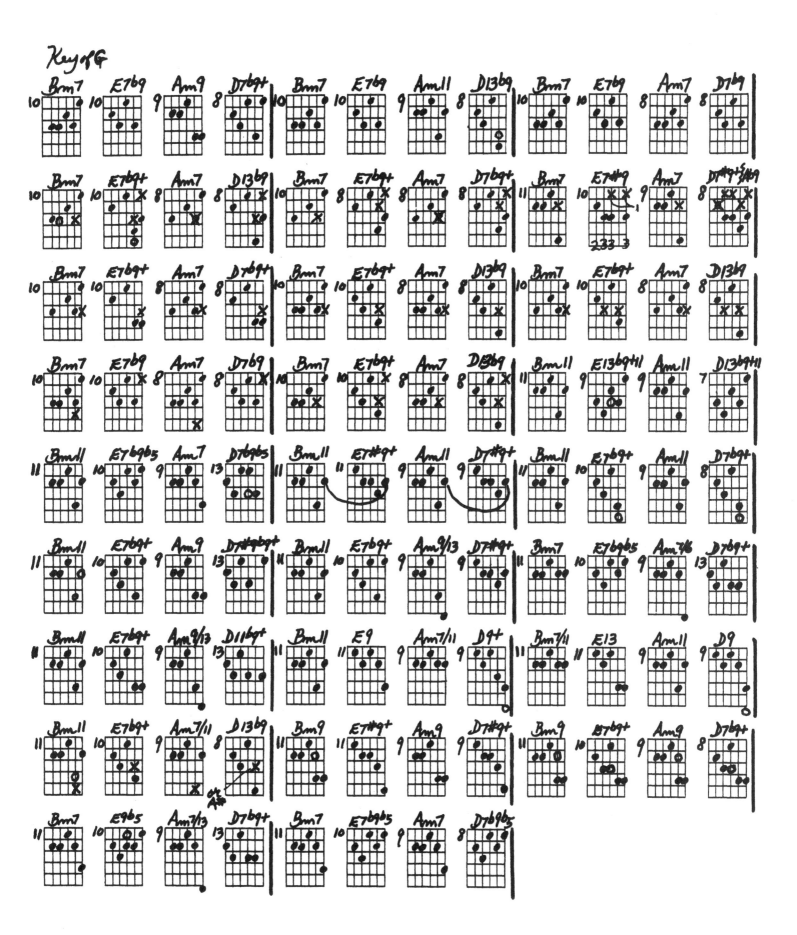

Key of E

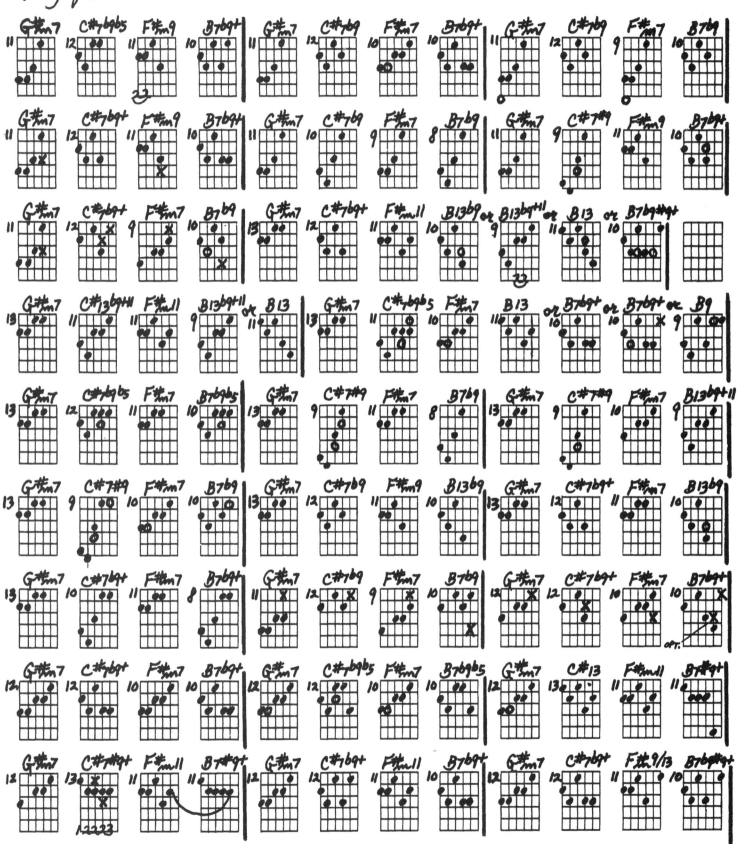

68

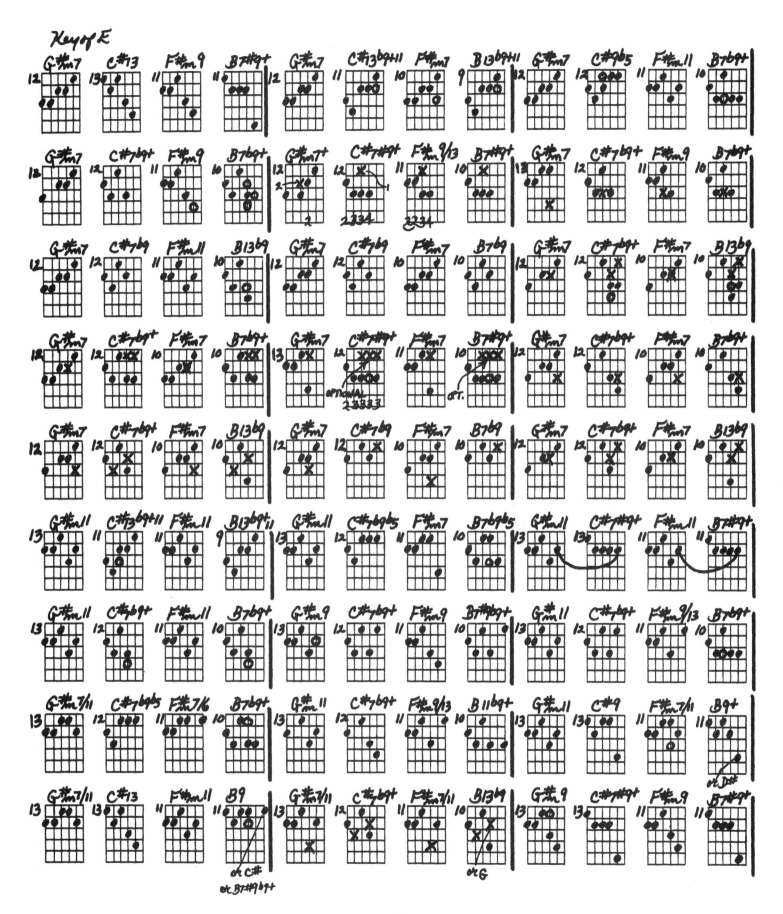

69

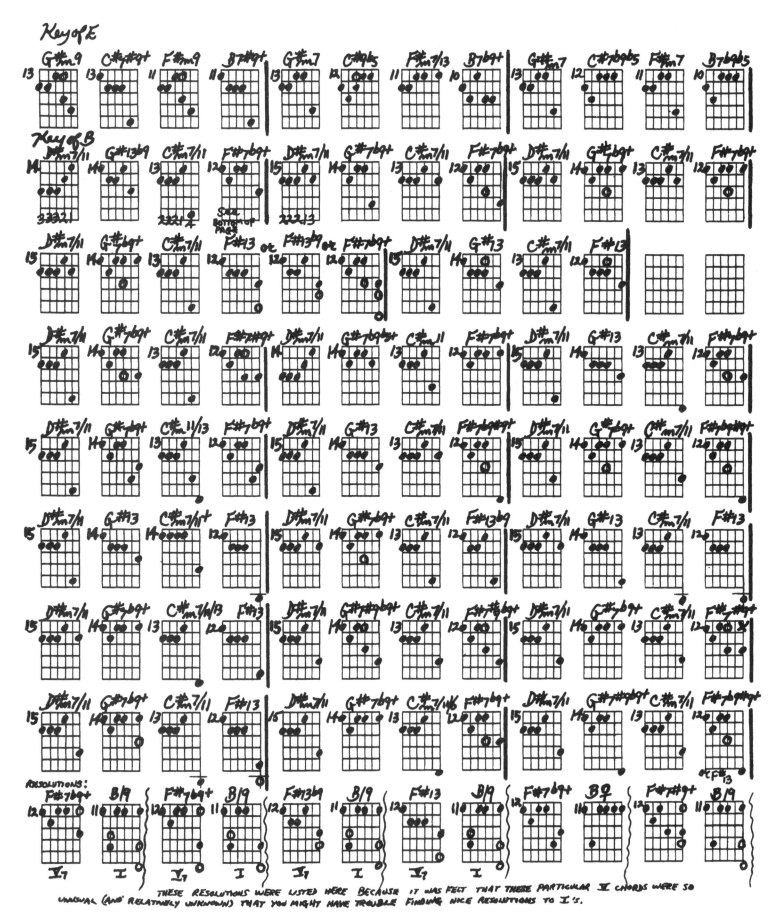

Key of E

Key of B

RESOLUTIONS:

THESE RESOLUTIONS WERE LISTED HERE BECAUSE IT WAS FELT THAT THESE PARTICULAR V CHORDS WERE SO UNUSUAL (AND RELATIVELY UNKNOWN) THAT YOU MIGHT HAVE TROUBLE FINDING NICE RESOLUTIONS TO I's.

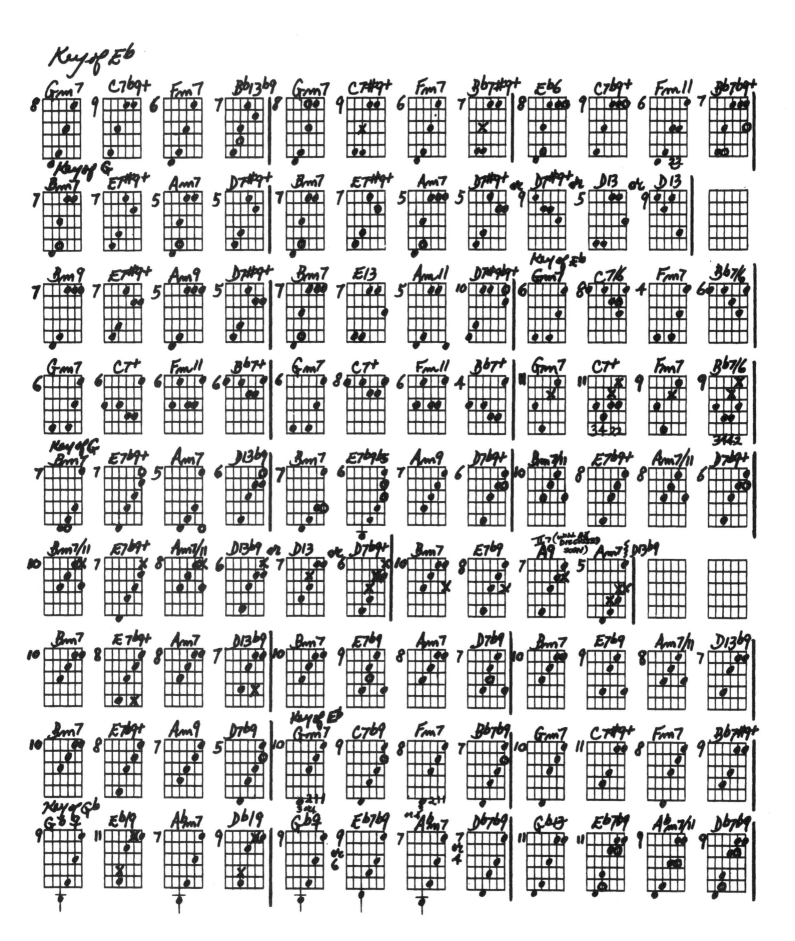

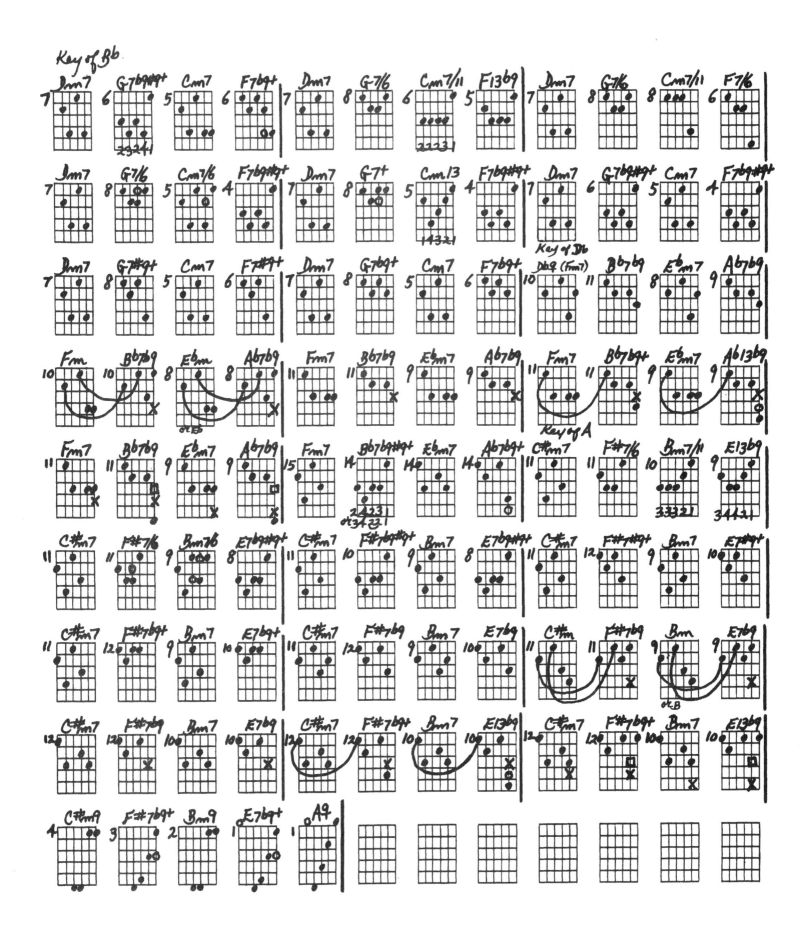

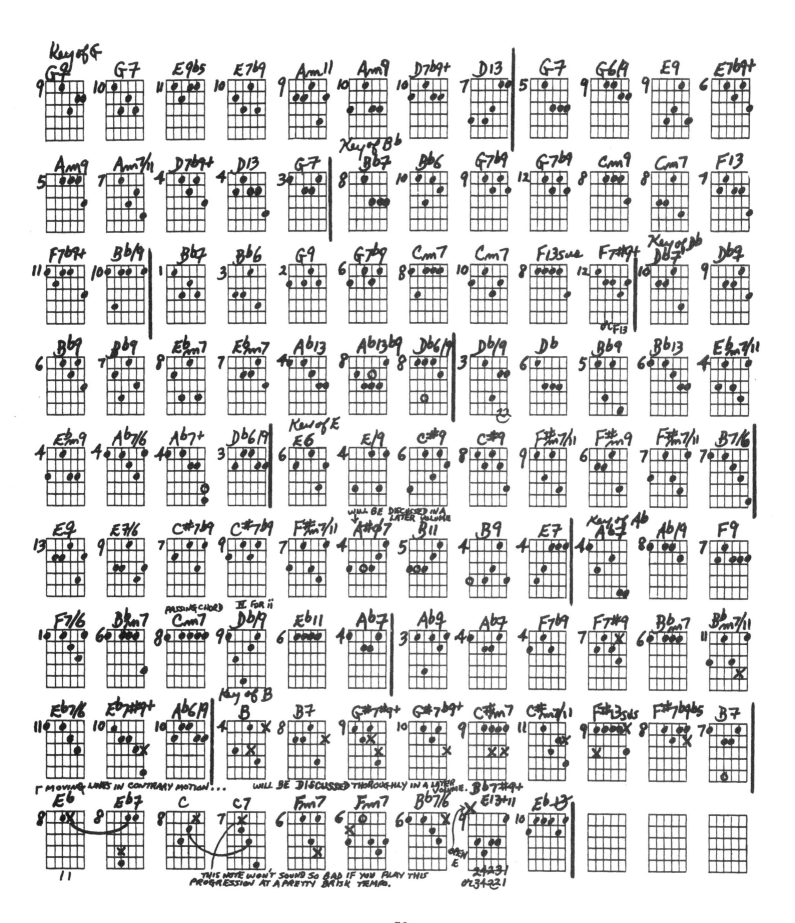

iii7 vi7 II7 V7 (and I7 vi7 II7 V7)

The next harmonic formula to concern us is going to be iii7 vi7 II7 V7 (sometimes I7 will be used in place of iii7). The quickest way for you to come up with some good examples of this progression is to go back to your iii7 vi7 ii7 V7 progressions and raise the 3rd (one fret higher) in the ii7 types, thereby making them II7's. If there are two 3rds in a ii7 type, try raising the 3rd that is the <u>lower</u> in pitch of the two, and just leave the other one alone; this will create a II7#9 chord in many cases. If you are dealing with a iim7/11 with its 11th in the soprano (highest pitch) then none of these ideas will work very well.

You may be wondering why we didn't derive the iii7 VI7 ii7 V7 progressions from the iii7 vi7 ii7 V7's in a similar fashion. Actually some of them were (that is, the 3rd was raised in the vi7, thereby creating the VI7), but most of them were derived in other ways, specifically to produce more desirable sounds. However, if you are curious, you may wish to go back to the iii7 vi7 ii7 V7's and raise the 3rd on the vi7, as explained above, just to see what you come up with.

Anyway, here are some other variations on iii7 vi7 II7 V7. Remember to try resolving the V7's to I, occasionally.

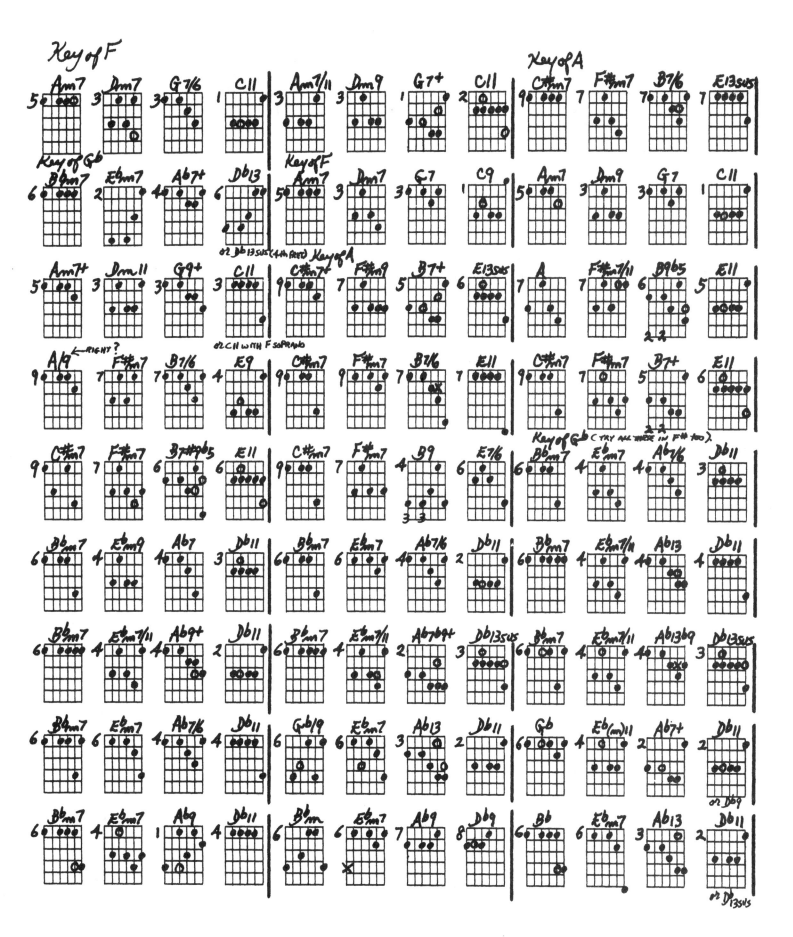

75

Key of G♭ (and do in F#)

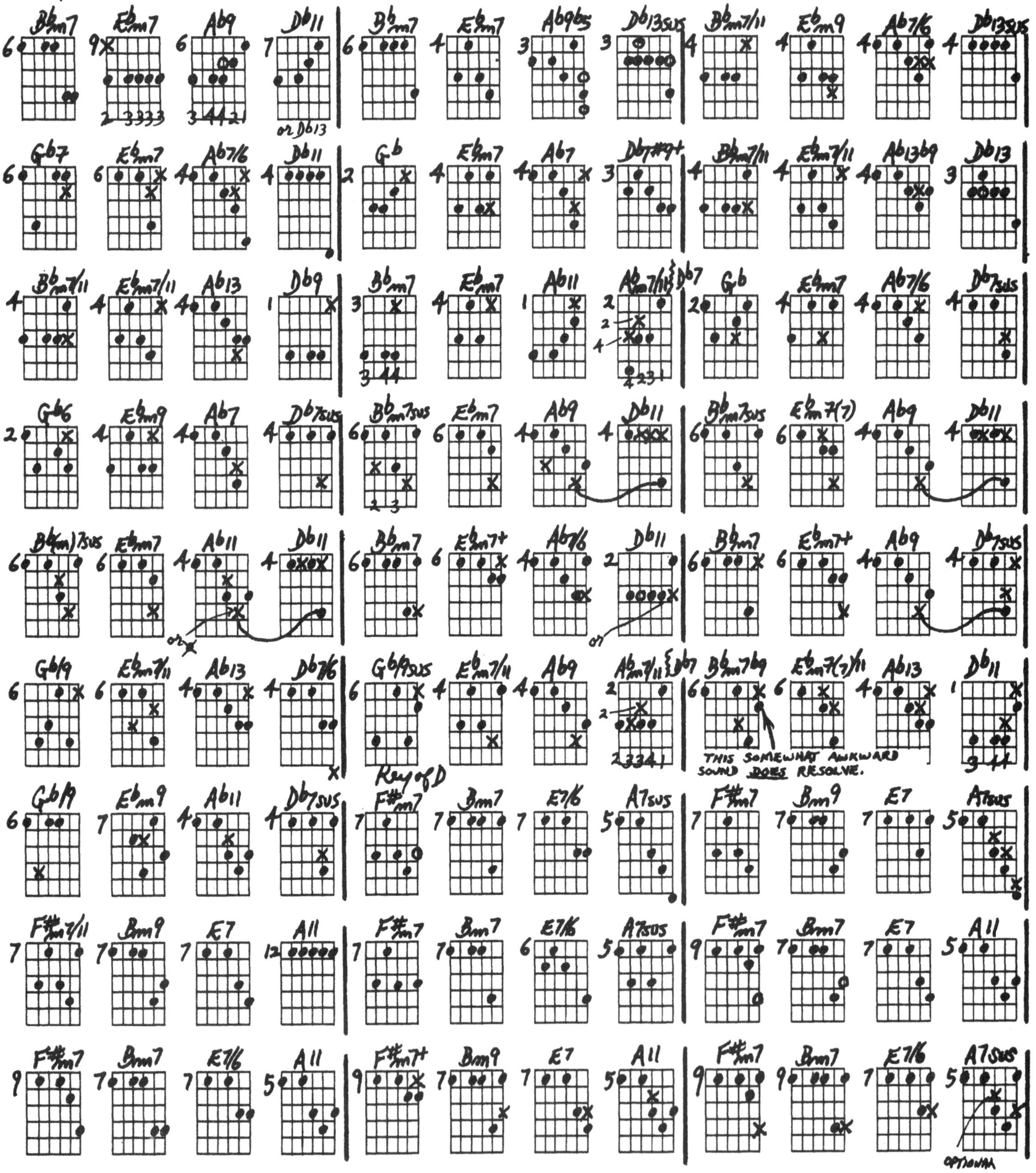

Key of D

76

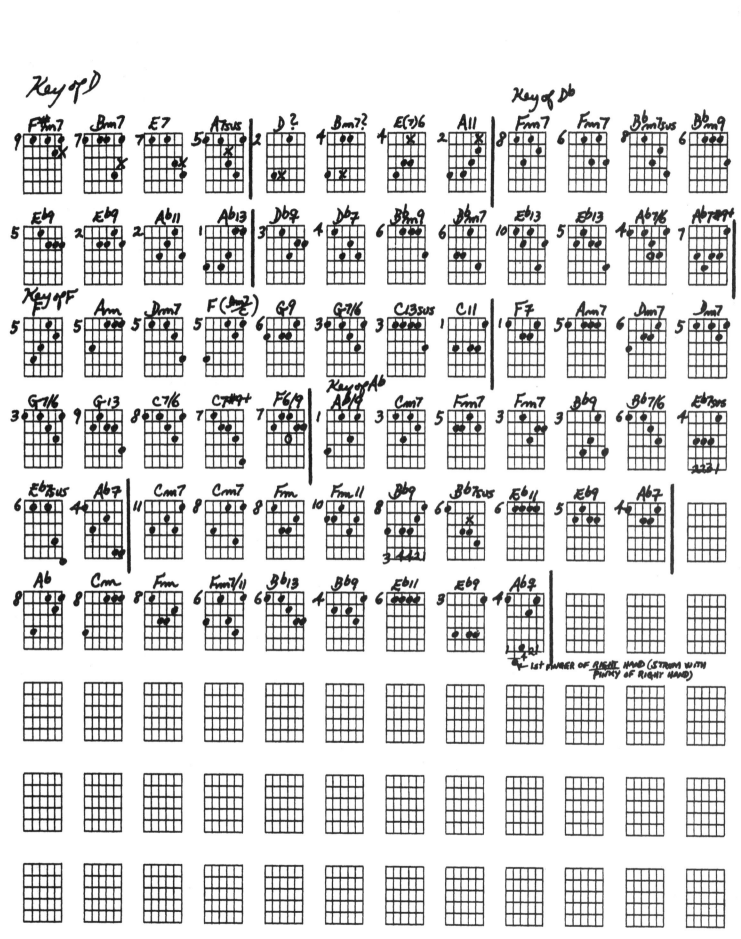

III7 VI7 II7 V7

The last harmonic formula we will deal with in this book is III7 VI7 II7 V7. There are many different examples given because there are many different attractive sounding chords that fit together well on this progression. These examples are organized, once again, according to which chord starts the progression.

A summary of starting forms is as follows:

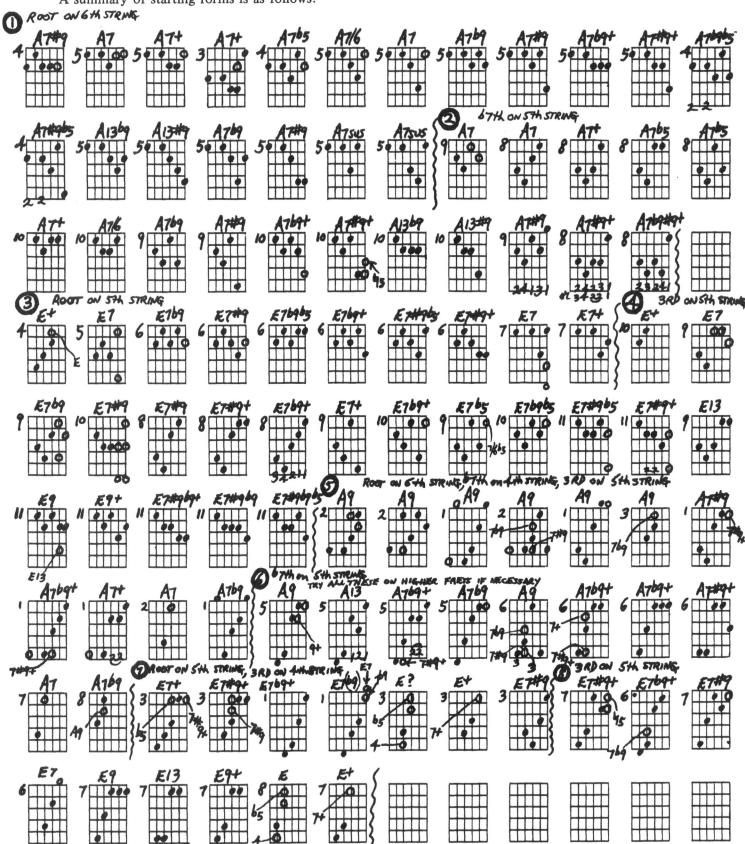

If you decide to skip around, and you run across a chord that you cannot find the right fingering for, the chances are great that the fingering was given earlier somewhere. Please remember, for your own good, this book is meant to be approached <u>in order</u>, <u>from the beginning to the end</u>.

Occasionally, you may wish to try using iii7 types in place of III7 types, or vi7 types in place of VI7 types. In many cases, either of these chords would sound very good — experiment and see what you think. Also, you might fool around with I7 or I7 for III7 (these are all common sounds).

Don't be alarmed if you get bored with this section though; this will probably be a normal reaction due to the fact that: 1) there are an incredible number of variations given, and 2) almost all of the examples use altered dominant 7th types (altered dominants are those with #9's, b9's, #5's, and b5's), which are very "spicy" chords. As mentioned earlier, given a little time and exposure, you will probably learn to enjoy these sounds even if you do not upon first hearing. But there is one qualification to this: Just as most people would not have a meal made up almost totally of spices, there is a good chance that you would not enjoy a piece of music in which almost every chord was an altered dominant, and yet, unfortunately, in one sense, this is what you will be hearing (the "piece" of music being one example after another) if you play through these examples for even a few minutes in a row. The solution? Take this whole section in small doses and add some of your favorite examples of these III7, VI7 II7 V7's to some of the more "normal" progressions you have already studied; the ear will accept altered chords more easily in most cases if they are prepared with sounds of a more normal, diatonic "major scaley" nature first.

EXAMPLES:

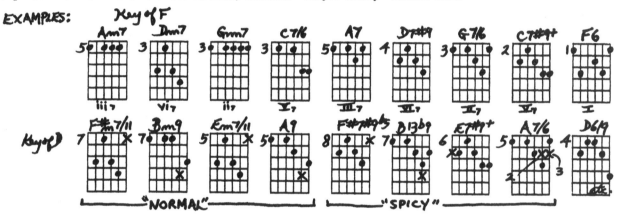

This type of technique (that is, of combining the consonant and dissonant types of progressions) is also fun for your ear because of the <u>contrast</u>; and it is good for you because it will get you into the spirit of combining shorter progressions in order to make longer progressions.

Don't forget to occasionally try resolving the V7's to I's.

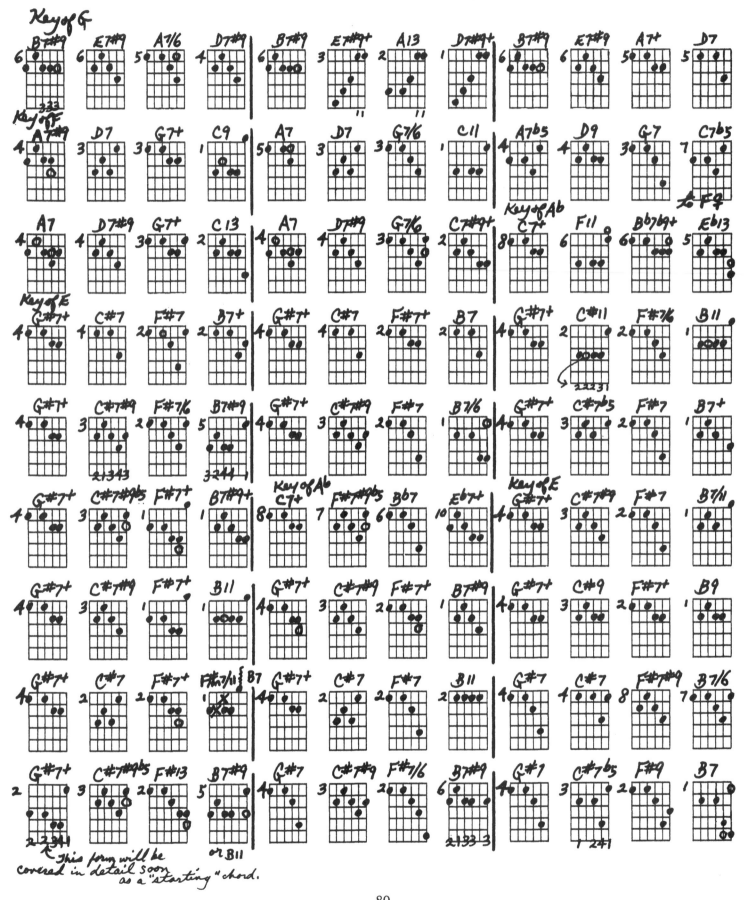

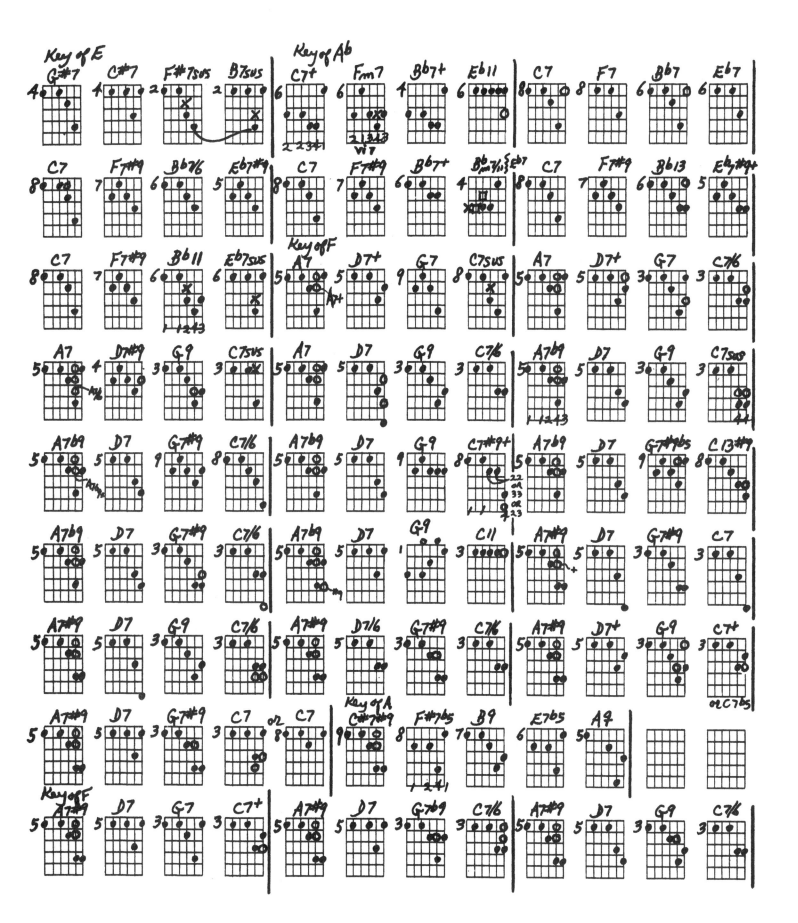

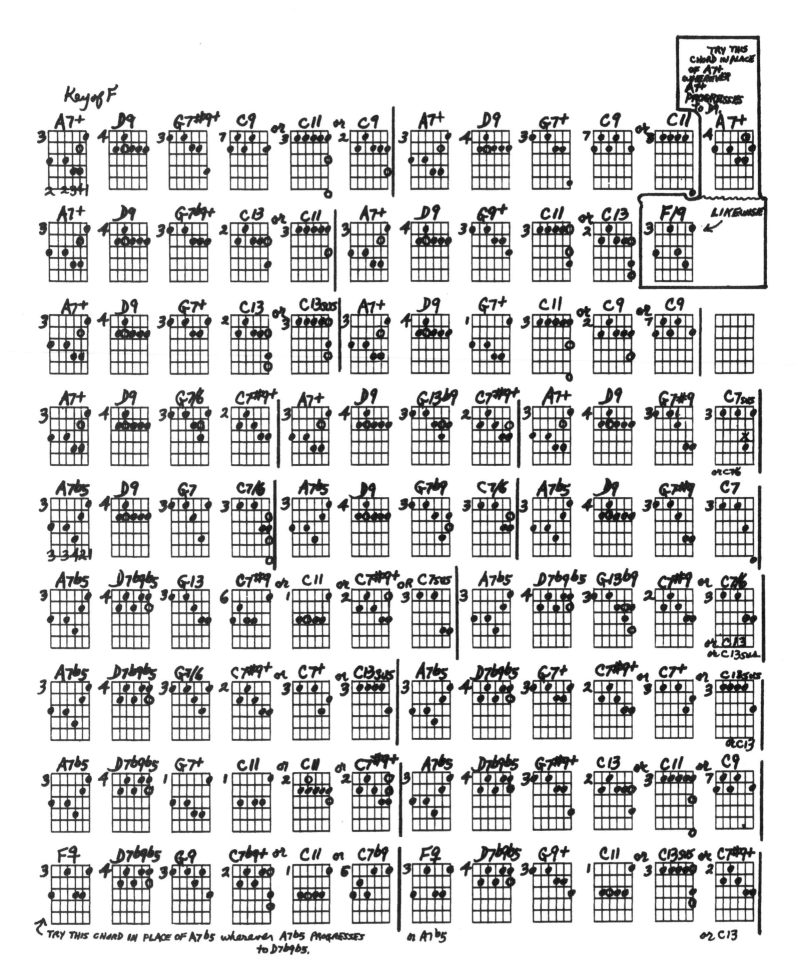

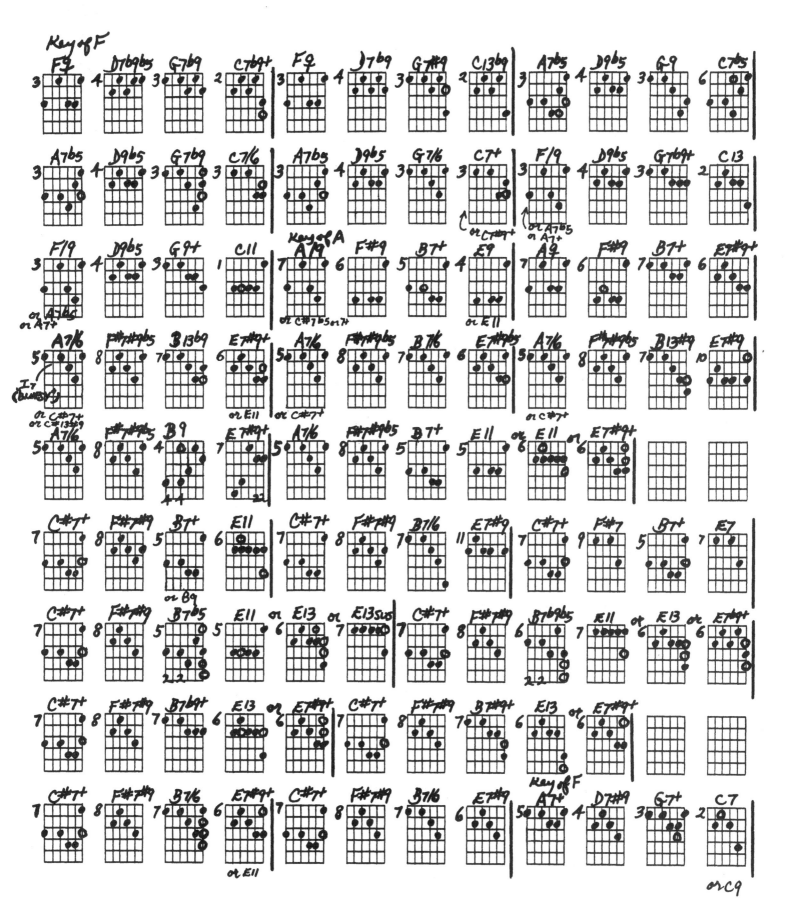

83

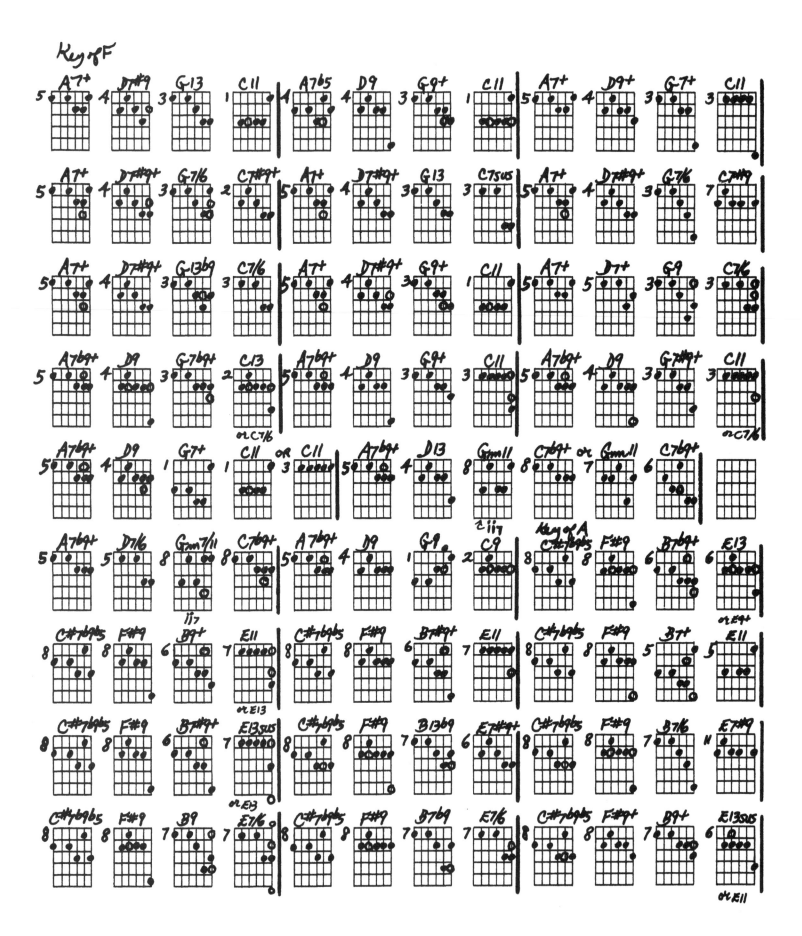

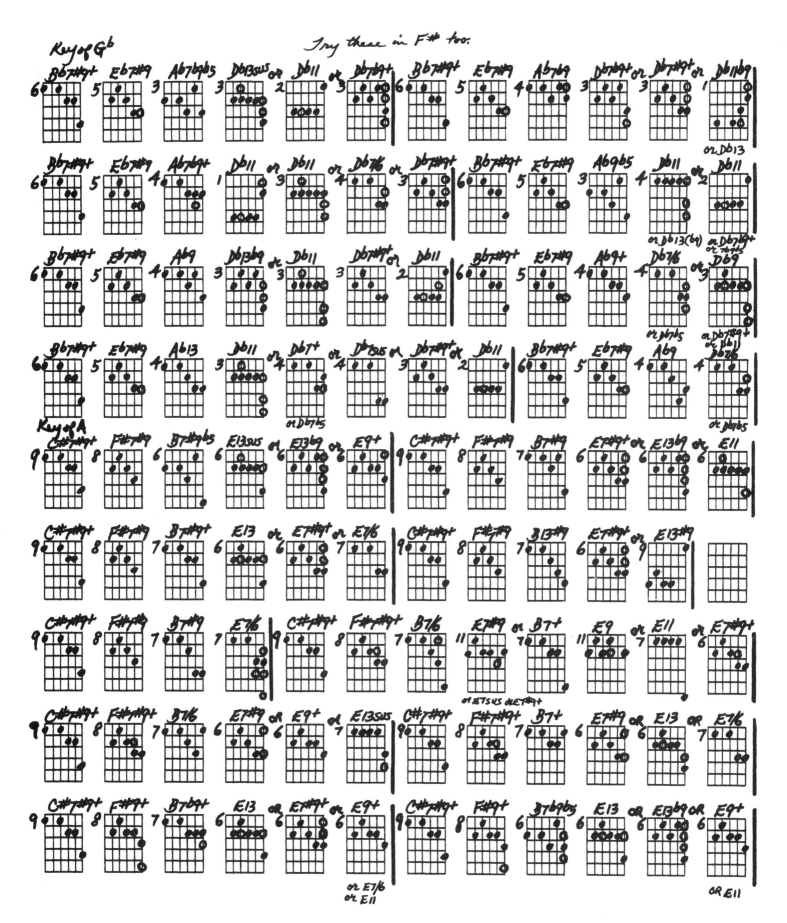

85

Key of A

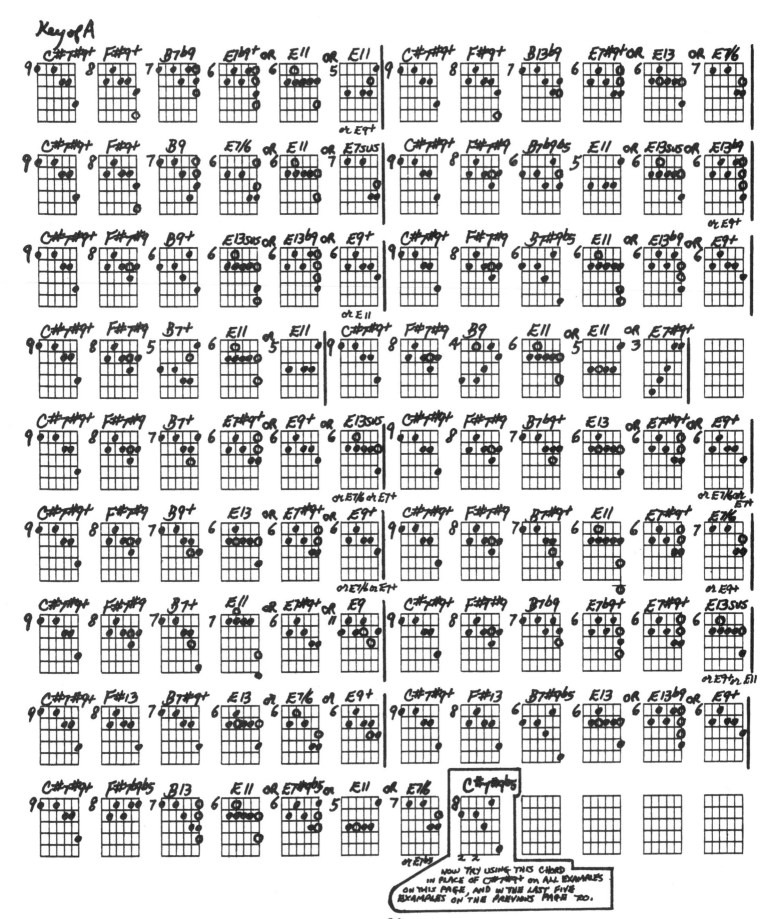

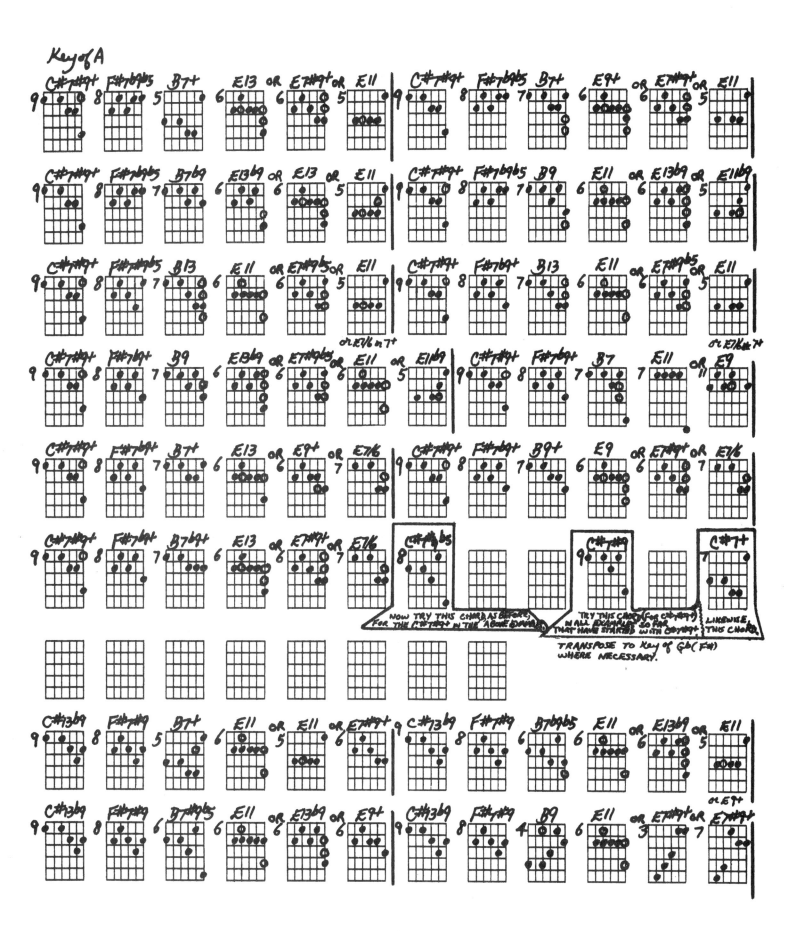

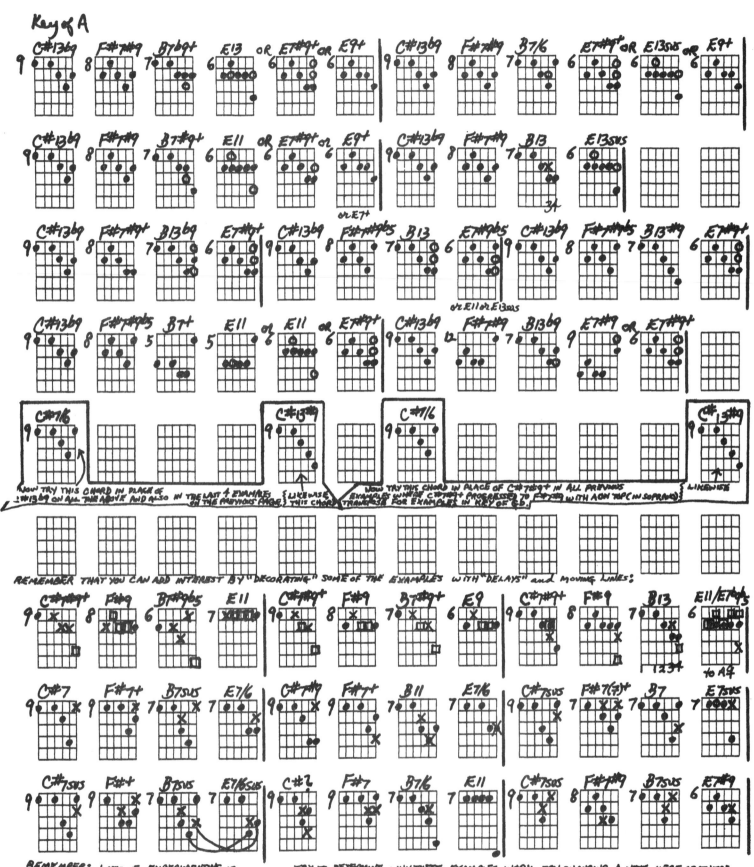

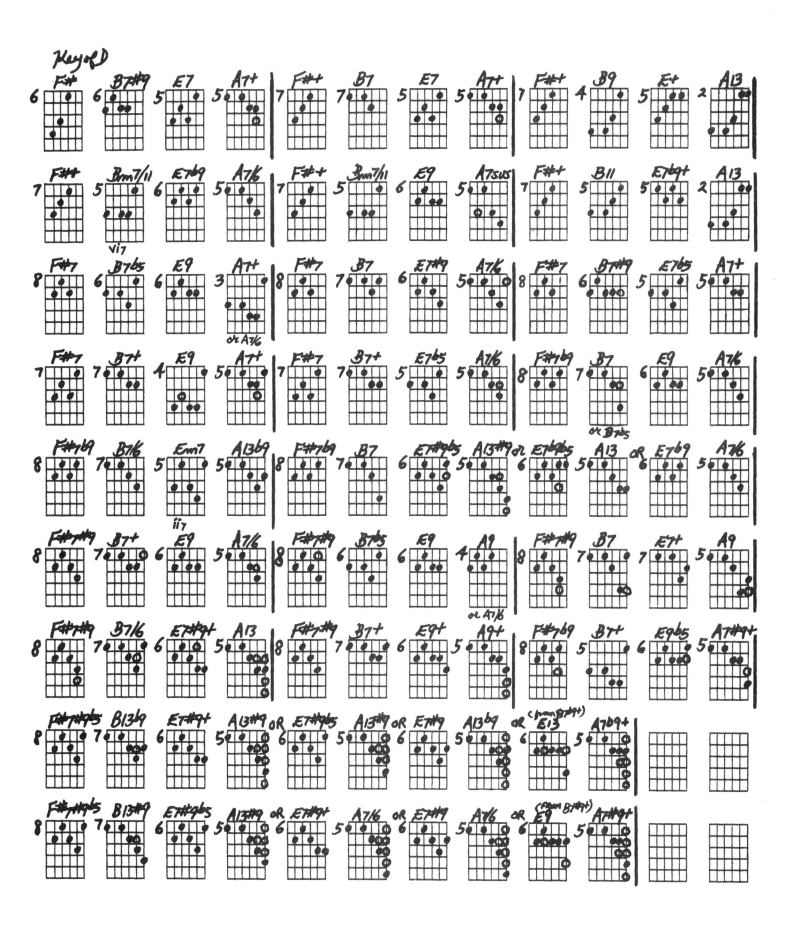

Key of D

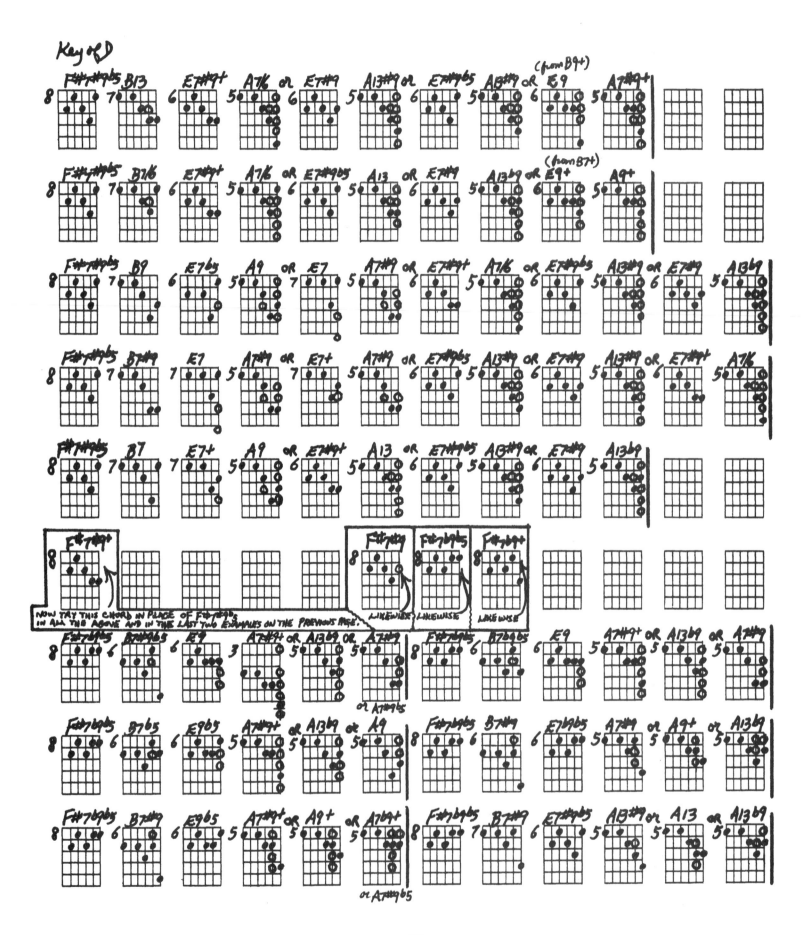

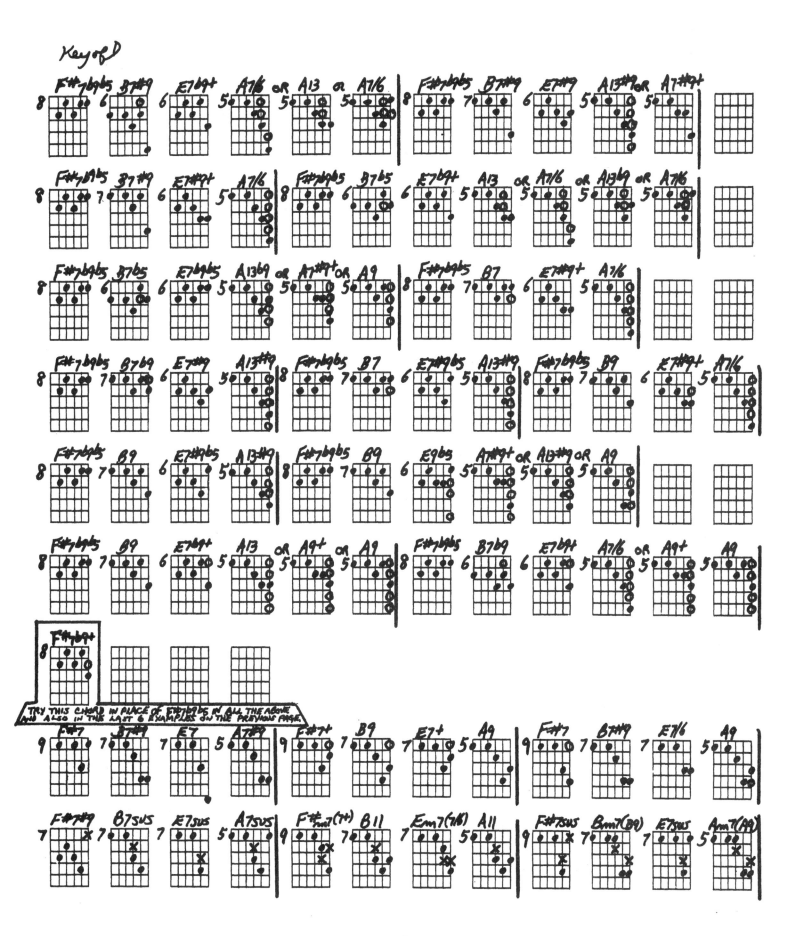

Key of D

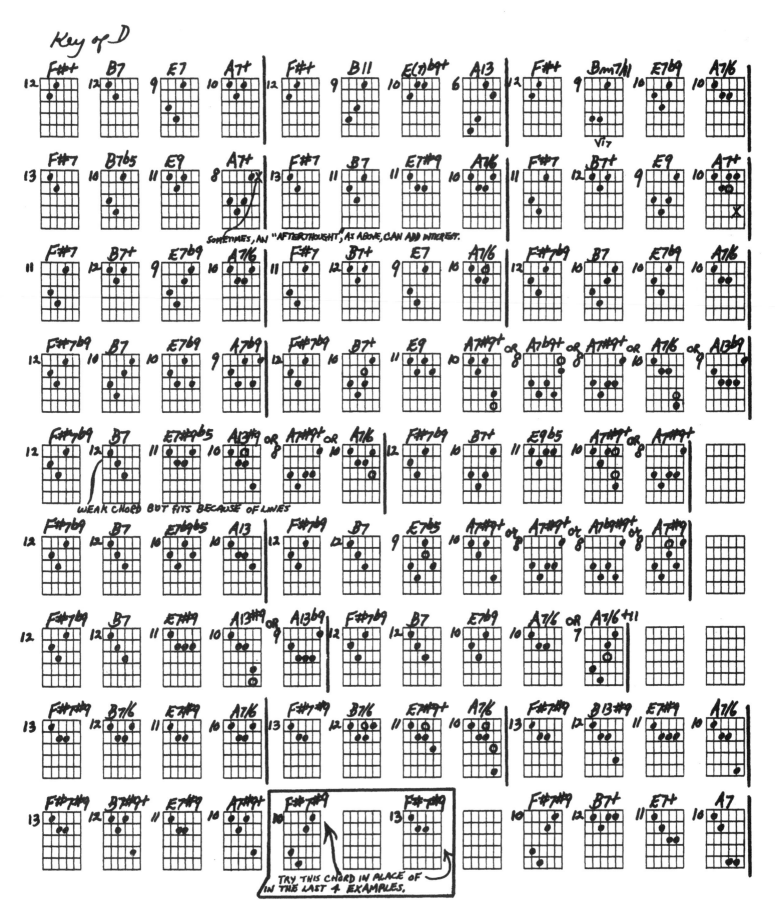

SOMETIMES, AN "AFTERTHOUGHT", AS ABOVE, CAN ADD INTEREST.

WEAK CHORD BUT FITS BECAUSE OF LINES

TRY THIS CHORD IN PLACE OF
IN THE LAST 4 EXAMPLES.

92

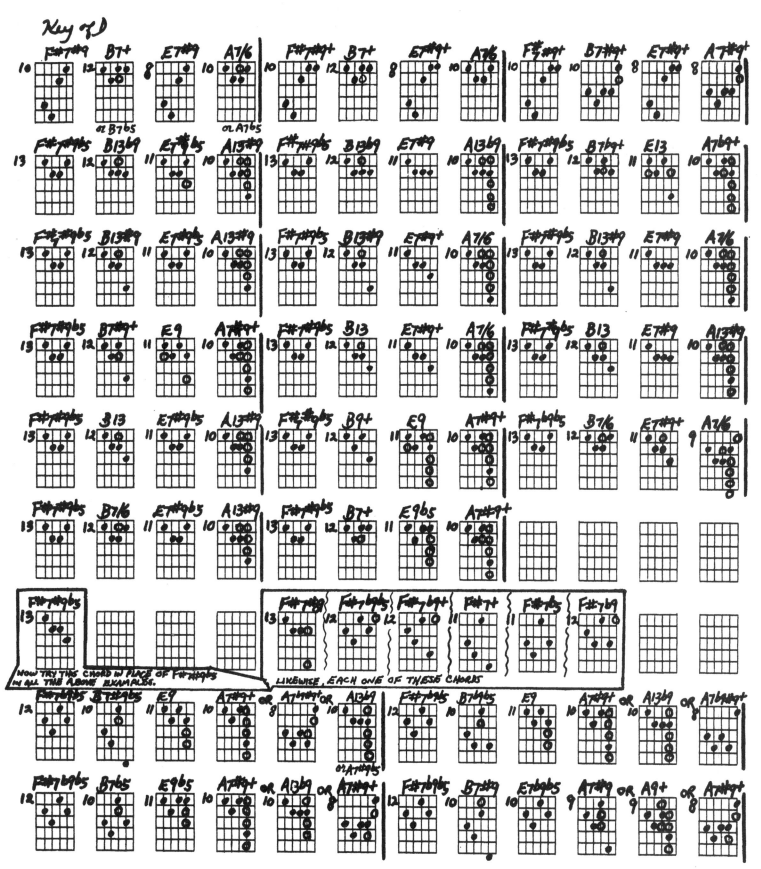

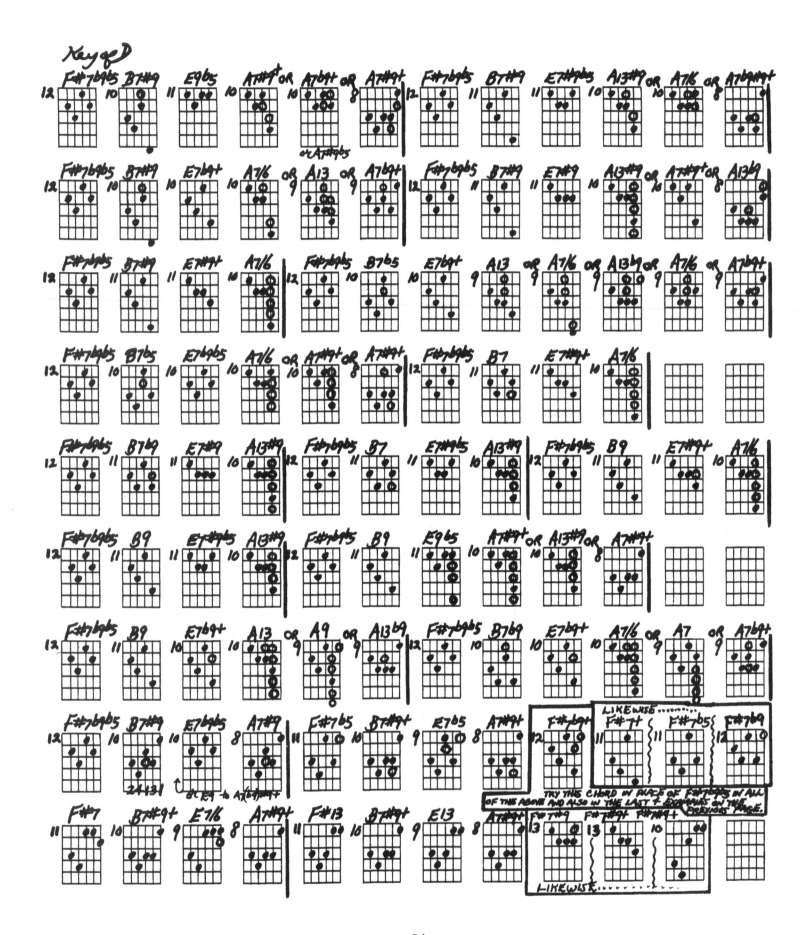

94

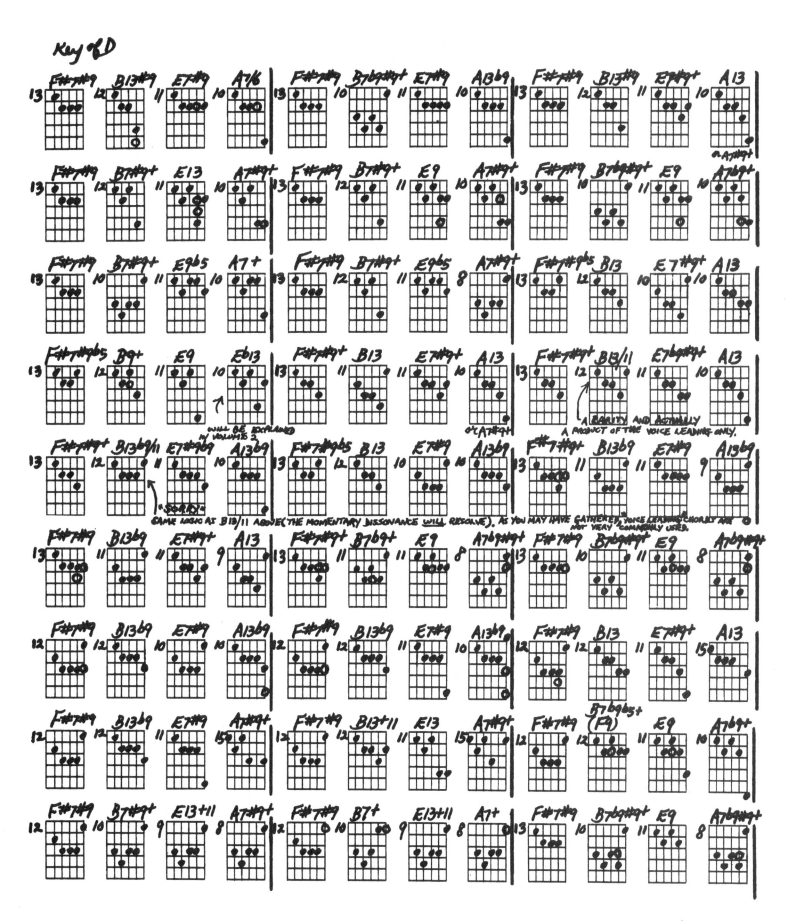

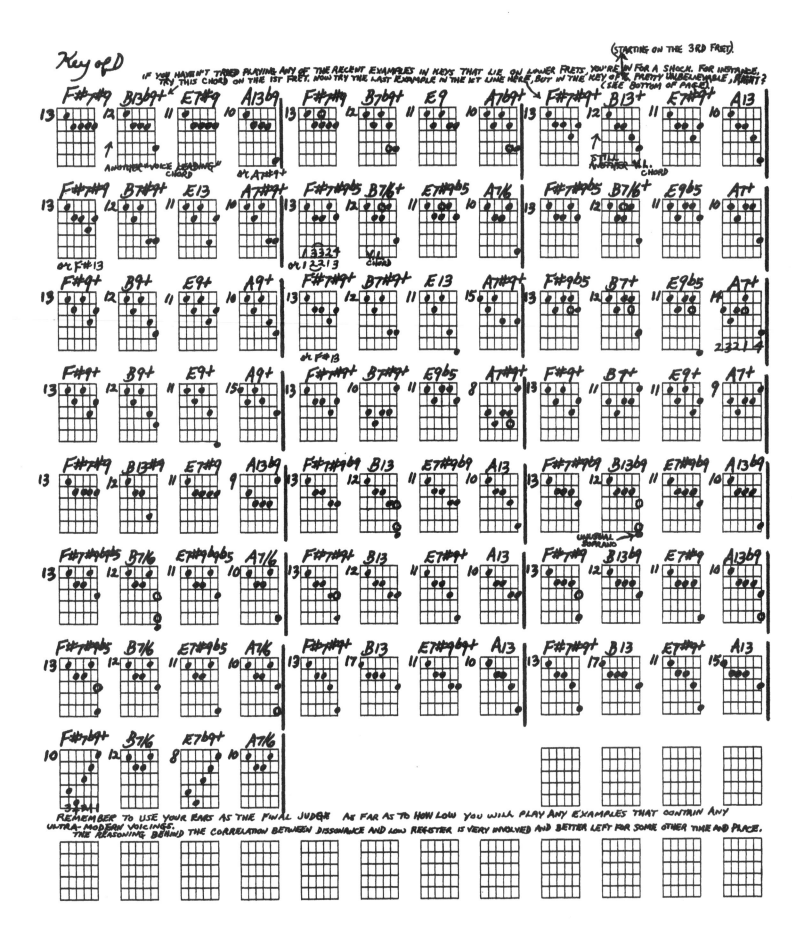

Key of D

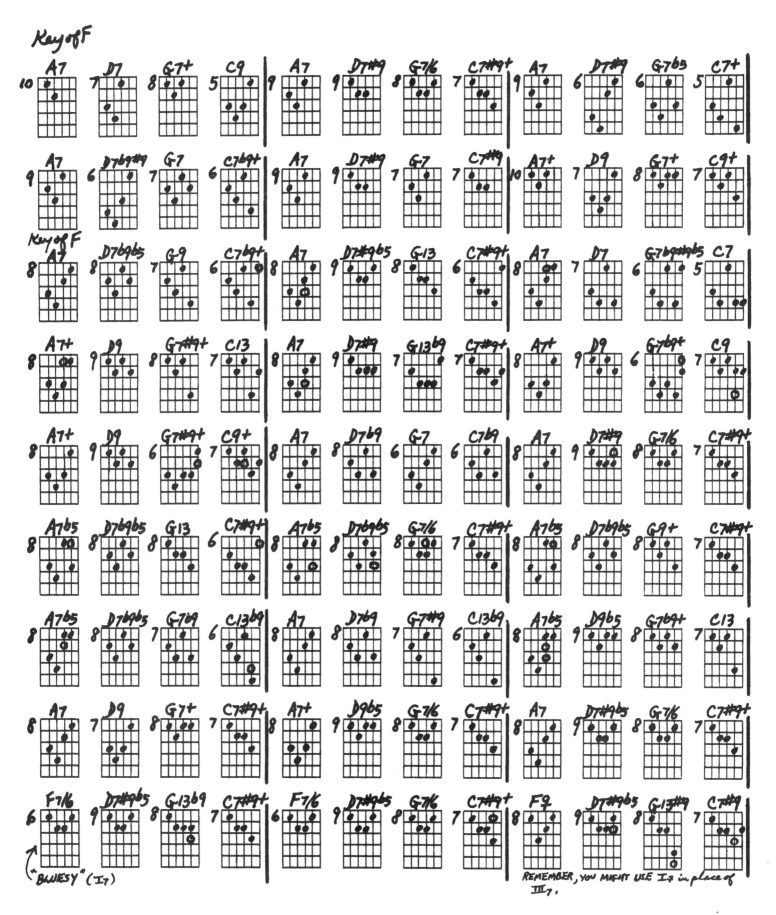

Key of F

97

Key of F

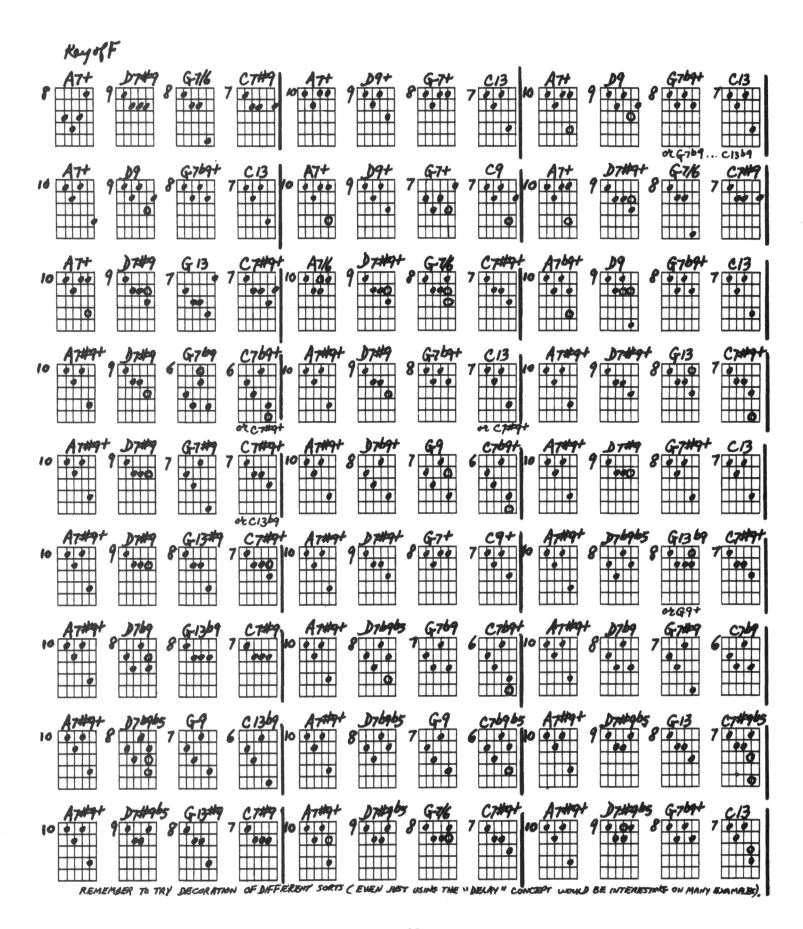

REMEMBER TO TRY DECORATION OF DIFFERENT SORTS (EVEN JUST USING THE "DELAY" CONCEPT WOULD BE INTERESTING ON MANY EXAMPLES).

98

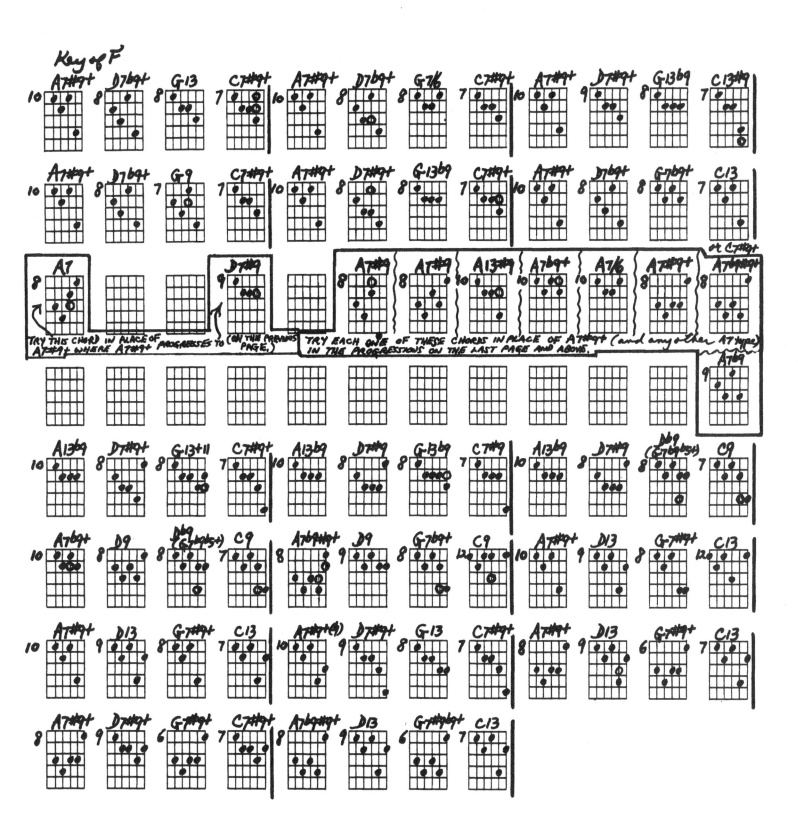

99

IF YOU HAVEN'T CUSSED ME OUT ALREADY, THE FOLLOWING PAGES WILL RECTIFY THIS PROBLEM.
YOU ARE GOING TO HAVE TO STRETCH ...., AND YOU WILL EVEN GET CRAMPS IN YOUR LEFT HAND, AS YOU NO DOUBT HAVE ALREADY.
ALL PART OF LEARNING TO CONTROL THE GUITAR INSTEAD OF HAVING IT CONTROL YOU.
REMEMBER: PATIENCE and DETERMINATION.

Key of G

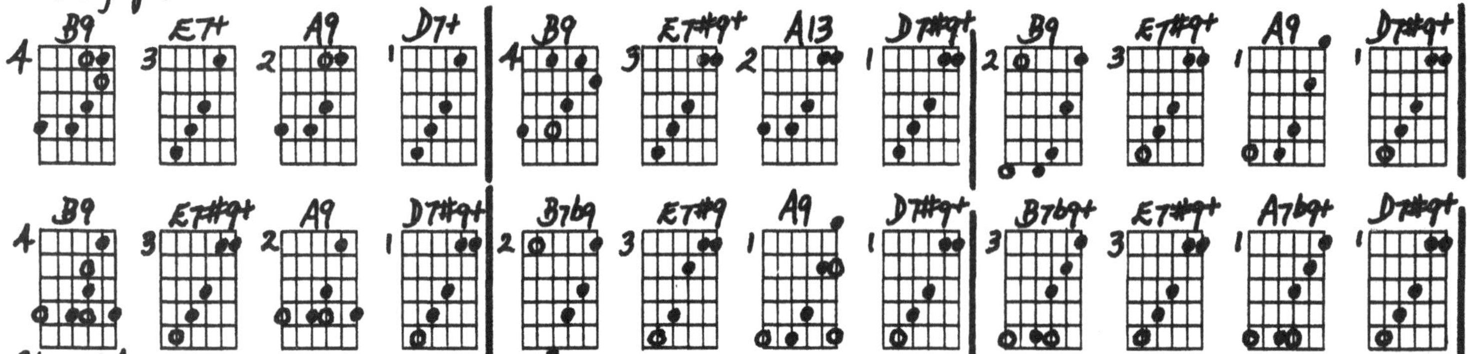

Key of A

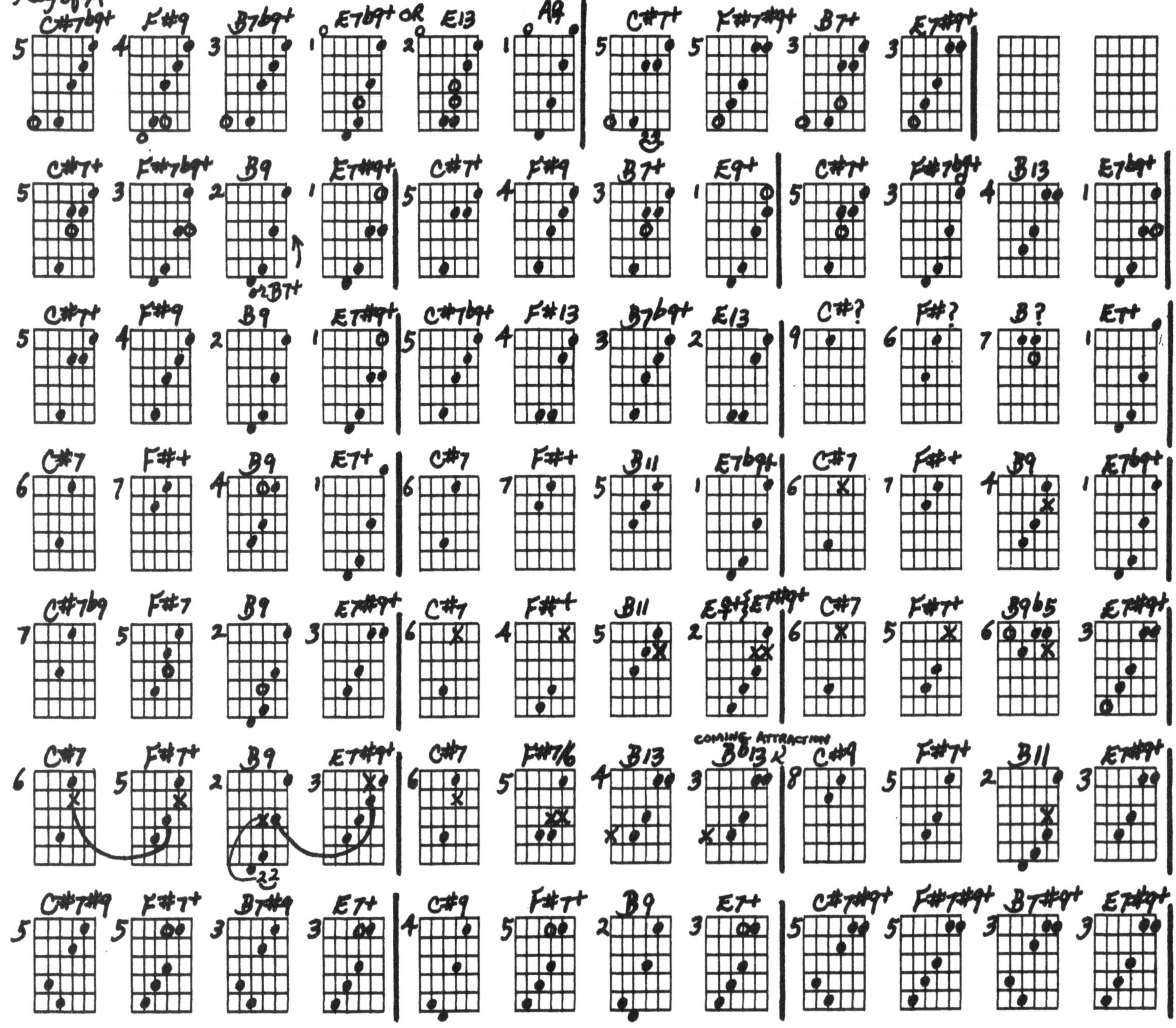

100

Key of A

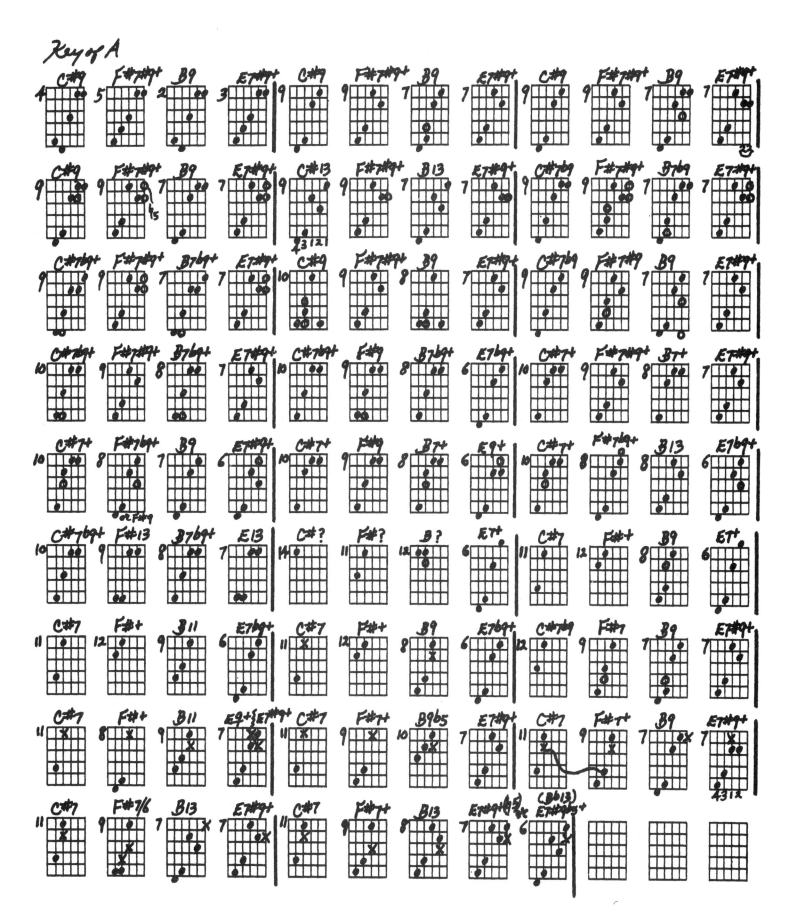

101

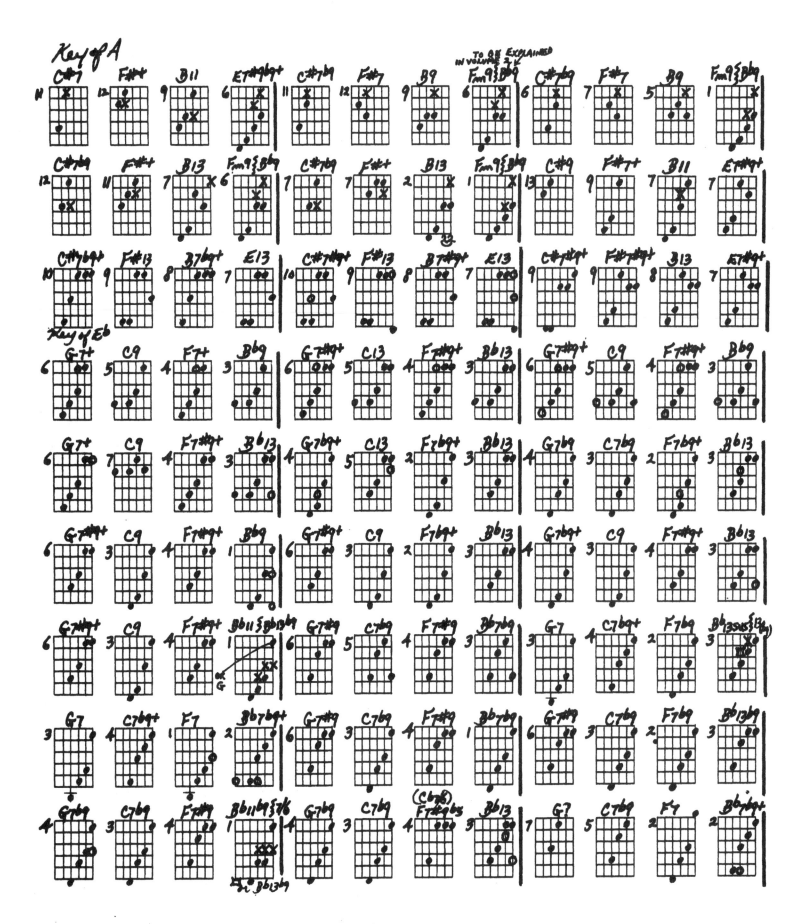

102

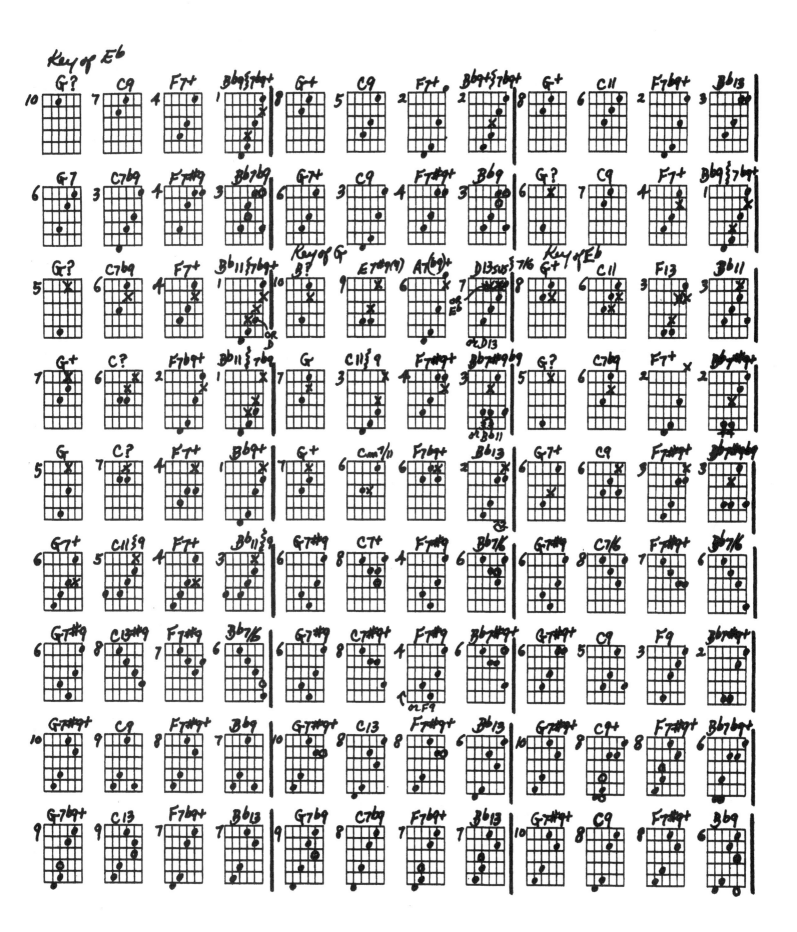

103

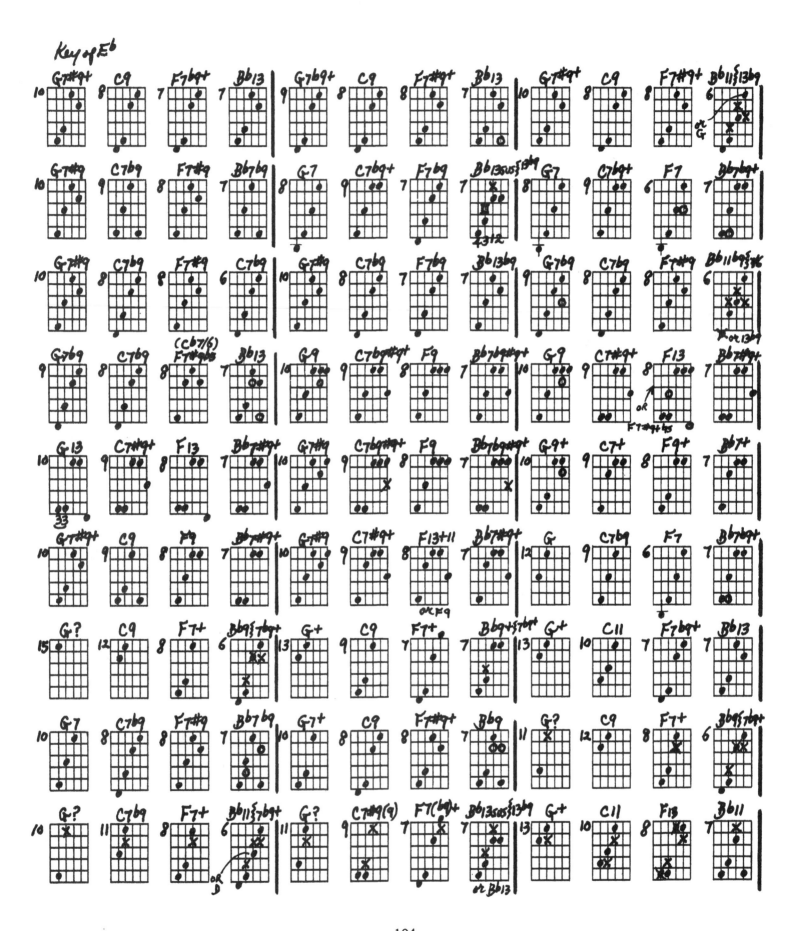

104

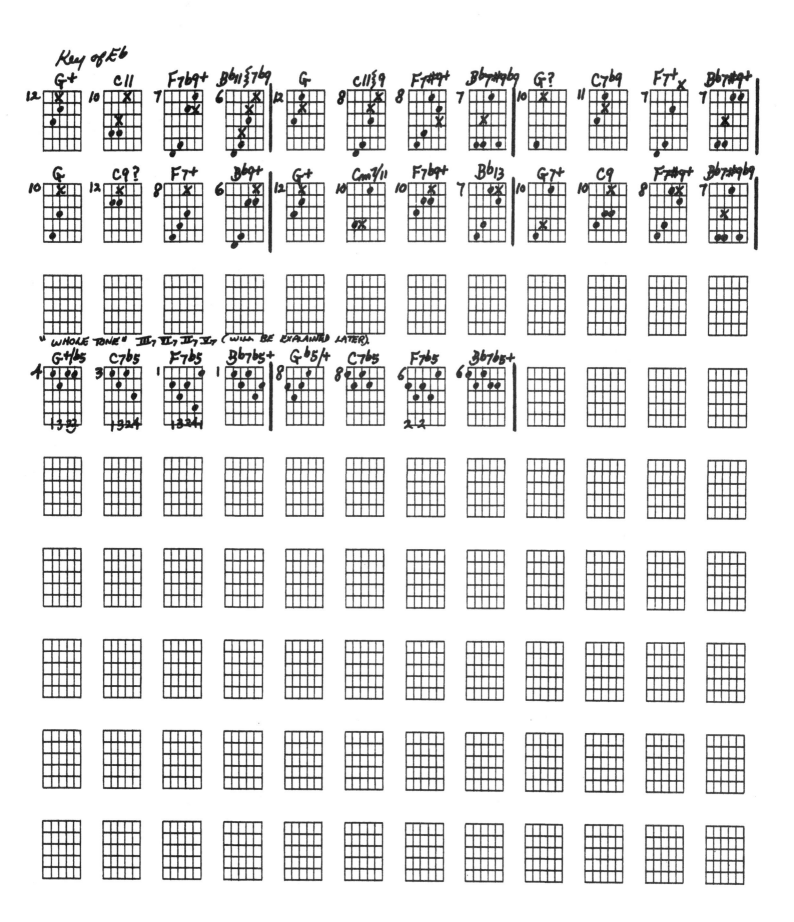

105

RECOMMENDED BOOKS

This list is far from complete, but it is a good starting place. Each book has something of value to offer; that doesn't mean that everything in each book is as well presented as it could be, but if you read enough different books given here, you will get a good overall picture of some of the most important facets of musical knowledge. It will mean a pretty sizable investment of money, but the increase in your musical understanding and abilities will compensate you many times over.

If you are fortunate enough to live in a city that has a store that specializes in sheet music and music text books, you will probably be able to see the majority of these books before you actually purchase them (also, you might check out college book stores and musical instrument stores).

I. BASIC MUSIC THEORY

TITLE	AUTHOR	PUBLISHER
Basic Materials in Music Theory	Paul O. Harder	Allyn and Bacon, Inc.
Foundations in Music Theory	Leon Dallin	Wadsworth Publishing Co., Inc.
Rudiments of Music	Jeannette Cass	Appleton-Century-Crofts
Rudiments of Music	John Castellini	W. W. Norton and Company, Inc.

II. BASIC MUSIC THEORY AND HARMONY

Practical Harmony	Hans Tischler	Allyn and Bacon, Inc.
Basic Principles of Music Theory	Joseph Brye	The Ronald Press Company (N.Y.)

III. HARMONY — An understanding of these books depends on an understanding of basic music theory.

Elementary Harmony } Advanced Harmony }	Robert W. Ottman	Prentice-Hall, Inc.
Harmony and Melody Volumes 1 and 2 (and Workbooks)	Elie Siegmeister	Wadsworth Publishing Co.
Harmonic Materials in Tonal Music Parts 1 and 2	Paul O. Harder	Allyn and Bacon, Inc.
Elementary Keyboard Harmony	Maurice Lieberman	W. W. Norton and Co., Inc.
Harmony	Walter Piston	W. W. Norton and Co., Inc.
Harmony: A Workbook in Fundamentals (to be used with Harmony by Walter Piston)	Paul Des Marais	W. W. Norton and Co., Inc.
The Contrapuntal Harmonic Technique of the 18th Century	Allen Irvine McHose	Appleton-Century-Crofts
Chromatic Harmony	Justine Shir-Cliff, Stephen Jay, Donald J. Rauscher	The Free Press, N.Y.
Harmony	Foote and Spalding	A. R. Schmidt Co. (Summy-Birchard Co.)
Figured Harmony at the Keyboard (Parts 1 & 2)	R. O. Morris	Oxford University Press
Harmony Book for Beginners	Preston Ware Orem	Theodore Presser Company
Applied Harmony (Books 1 and 2)	George A. Wedge	G. Schirmer
Elementary Harmony	William J. Mitchell	Prentice-Hall
Harmony for Ear, Eye and Keyboard	Arthur E. Heacox	Oliver Ditson Co.

TITLE	AUTHOR	PUBLISHER

IV. MODERN HARMONY – Basic theory understanding is also necessary to cope easily with these books.

Modern Harmonic Technique (Vol. 2 only)	Gordon Delamont	Kendor Music, Inc.
Developing a Complete Harmonic Technique	Mitchell Farber	Mitchell Farber, 42 William St., Ossining, N.Y. 10562
Popular and Jazz Harmony	Daniel A. Ricigliano	Donato Music Publishing Co.

V. GUITAR BOOKS

The Guitarist's Harmony	Robert Lilienfeld, Basil Cimino	Belwin Mills Publishing Corp.
Modern Guitar Method	George M. Smith	Guitarists' Publications, Hollywod, Ca.
Chord Chemistry	Ted Greene	D. Z. Publications
Original Guitar Solos	George Van Eps	Plymouth Music Co., Inc.
Jazz Guitar Method, Volume 2	Ronny Lee	Mel Bay Publications

VI. NOTE READING FOR GUITAR

Sight to Sound	Leon White	D. Z. Publications
Mel Bay Modern Guitar Methods, Books 1-7	Mel Bay	Mel Bay Publishing
Solo Guitar Playing	Fredrick M. Noad	Collier Books
Modern Method for Guitar, Vol. 1-3	William Leavitt	Berklee Press Publications
Classic Guitar Technique, Vol. 1, 2	Aaron Shearer	Franco Colombo Publications
Mel Bay Classic Guitar Method, Vol. 1-3	Mel Bay	Mel Bay Publications

VII. NOTE READING

Learn to Read Music	Howard Shanet	Simon and Schuster

VIII. COUNTERPOINT – Here you are best off with a background in theory <u>and</u> harmony.

Counterpoint } Counterpoint Workbook }	Kent Wheeler Kennan	Prentice-Hall, Inc.
Essentials of 18th Century Counterpoint	Neale B. Mason	Wm. C. Brown Co. Publishers
Tonal Counterpoint in the Style of the 18th Century	Ernst Krenek	Boosey & Hawkes, Inc.
Elementary Counterpoint	Percy Goetschius	G. Schirmer, Inc.
The Technique and Spirit of Fugue	George Oldroyd	Oxford University Press

Most of the books in this list (with the exception of Sections V and VI) are geared for the keyboard, not the guitar. But much of this information can be transferred over to guitar (if you don't know how to do this, you might look at the end of Section 14 of Chord Chemistry), or this might be a good incentive for you to learn a little piano, which should prove to be very helpful.